REPEAT OFFENDERS

50 ESSAYS REFLECTING A RECORD OF 'PRIOR CONVICTIONS' COMPILED FROM A QUARTER CENTURY OF PETTY PUNDITRY

BILL BONVIE

DIVERTIR
PUBLISHING
Salem, NH

REPEAT OFFENDERS

Bill Bonvie

Copyright © 2014 Bill Bonvie

All rights reserved. No portion of this publication may be reproduced or transmitted in any form or by any means, electronic or mechanical, including photocopy, recording, or any information storage and retrieval system, without prior permission from the publisher, except by a reviewer who may quote brief passages in a review.

Edited by Laura Jamison

Cover design by Laura Jamison

Published by Divertir Publishing LLC
PO Box 232
North Salem, NH 03073
http://www.divertirpublishing.com/

ISBN-13: 978-1-938888-07-6
ISBN-10: 1-938888-07-3

Library of Congress Control Number: 2014950251

Printed in the United States of America

Dedication

*This book is dedicated to Linda,
my amazing little sister and secret weapon,
and to the memory of my mother, Pauline Comanor,
and my grandparents, Harry and Fanny Comanor.*

TABLE OF CONTENTS

Backword .... *i*

ILLUSION INTRUSIONS

A career nearly nipped in the bud by an encounter with 'Mr. Quaker' 1
Starving for attention 5
How an itsy-bitsy incongruity can unravel a 'gospel truth' 9
Notes from the anti-Condoist underground 13
Making a monkey business connection 19
Christmas: the whole schmear 23
Elevating the 'nanny state' to supernanny nation status 27
Industry in the FDA's corner 31

THEORIES OF EVOLUTION

Taking credit for an idea that flew (and could fly a whole lot higher) 37
A brave new world of pharmacological possibilities 41
Doing justice to the presidency 45
Guns and butter 49
Smoking out new business 51
Exporting rubbish 55

TRIALS AND ERRORS

A lesson in civility 59
Warding off the underworld 61
Senseless violence and sensible values 65
Cracking down on petty philanthropy 69
Guarding your future 73

ANECDOTAL ANOMALIES

Back on the front burners of history 79
The two-cent refund that redeemed my sense of self-worth 83
Inadvertent Internet identity theft, part I 85
Inadvertent Internet identity theft, part II 89
Segregation of lawyers: it's no joke 93

FEAR FABRICATIONS

There's nothing like fear itself to see us through fearful times 99
Postal paranoia: rethinking what is and is not a 'suspect piece of mail' 103
Almanac alert: one small step from satire 107

OBJECTS OF MY OBJECTION

Taking the offensive 113
If this is 'news', that sure is news to me 117
A blow to an egalitarian ego 121
Summertime blues — an underrated malady 125
Most of all, you've got to hide it from the kids 129

CULTURED PERILS

Consumer fraud of the 'verse' kind 133
A long record of lamentable lyrics 137
Overkilling a mockingbird in Muskogee 141
Last words on McVeigh's last words 147
The blinding demise of a superstar 151
Filmdom's 'finest' in free fall 153

WRITING WRONGS

The authorship authenticity gap 159
A prize piece of prevarication 163
Abbreviation abuse: a 'capital' offense 167

OBSERVATION PLATFORMS

'Slip Sliding Away' toward oblivion 173
A pitch for 'home teams' to live up to their billing 177
Space travel just isn't what it used to be 181
Raining on our charade 185
The Constitution, not the flag, is what needs protecting 187
In defense of our God-given right to 'sue the bastards' 189
A lesson in reality from today's 'Mad Men' 193
A new bumper-sticker sentiment for situations when push comes to shovel 197
An official stamp of approval for an unofficial Statue of Liberty 201

Acknowledgments 203
About the Author 205

BACKWORD*

When I first entered the newspaper business at the callow age of 21, the thing I found most appealing about it was the mantle of "objectivity" it provided, which for me afforded a kind of protection not unlike Harry Potter's cloak of invisibility. In fact, it had the effect of making me feel a bit like some extraterrestrial being with no apparent opinions of my own on the various earthly issues and controversies I was assigned to cover. I was thus free to go about interviewing individuals of every stripe, including those I might ordinarily have regarded as repugnant (e.g., a "king kleagle" of the Ku Klux Klan), and do so with a straight face, never seeming to take sides, even when, from my unseasoned perspective, there was only one side with any legitimacy.

The problem was I did have opinions—and, like anything severely suppressed and muzzled, they were always on the verge of open rebellion (especially as I came to learn more and more about how the Real World operated). The chance for those bottled-up convictions to break free finally came in 1982 when I left the unyielding impartiality of the newsroom to work as a freelance copywriter for Connecticut advertising agencies. Rather than expressing them in a straightforward way, I tried a tongue-in-cheek approach, portraying then-President Ronald Reagan as a secret Soviet agent bent on discrediting capitalism (this incidentally, was well before his "comradeship" with Mikhail Gorbachev):

"It now appears that the much-maligned House Un-American Activities Committee of the 1950s was right all along when it tried to sound the alarm about the extent of the ideological menace within the show business community."

I subsequently sold the piece to the op-ed page of *The Hartford Courant*, and thus became hooked on a life of petty punditry I have been more or less enmeshed in ever since.

REPEAT OFFENDERS

All 50 essays contained in this book are selected from a much larger assortment; all published over the past 25 years on the op-ed and commentary pages of various newspapers, with subsequent developments noted whenever it seemed appropriate to include them. During that time, more than a few readers seem to have been offended by the ideas I've expressed in such dissertations, judging from many of the letters to the editor they elicited. But that's as it should be, because if no one were riled by any of my views, they wouldn't be worth venting—let alone repeating. And while some of the issues I've addressed have been put to rest, I have no doubt what I've had to say about others may still be capable of re-offending, because the basic bones of contention somehow never quite managed to stay buried.

It goes without saying most pundits have some sort of an ideological ax to grind, causing opinion-page editors to attempt to "balance" the contributions they feature on any given day. (And, as you may have already ascertained, mine tend to be a left-handed ax, although on certain issues—especially cultural ones—I can become ambidextrous.) But if you want to know my opinion of what really drives the continuous compulsion to go on record with one's opinions—the thing anybody who does so on a professional basis really desires—I would venture it's the supreme satisfaction of being able to say "I told you so." The down side of this, however, is the way it reveals how little influence contemporary pundits actually possess (including those sages who, unlike myself, are blessed with syndication), as opposed to those of years past who actually had the ability to sway policy decisions.

One example of what I'm talking about was an essay of mine that appeared in *The SandPaper*, (a weekly based in Long Beach Island, N.J. to which I have contributed commentary for more than two decades) back in 2005, which ran under the headline, "Florida Sets Perilous New Preemption Precedent"—one of many, for various reasons, I chose not to include in this book. The piece was one I opened discussing two then-current episodes in which seemingly "good people" had been implicated in fatal gun violence, including one reported in the *Philadelphia Inquirer* involving a man who was shot upon answering his doorbell by a former coworker whose apparent motive was the victim once told a joke that offended him (a case I noted was strikingly similar to a fictional scenario envisioned by author Kurt Vonnegut in his novel *Slaughterhouse Five*). I then went on to note that on the same day that was being given prominent media coverage, "yet another news report made it clear when it comes to the act of deliberately shooting someone, a terrible precedent was indeed already being set." I was referring to the passage of Florida's "stand your ground" law, which I thought should cause "visitors to the Sunshine State (to) best beware of Floridians bearing arms. That's because anything you say or do might in any way be perceived as threatening to a Florida resident could quite conceivably result in your quite legally being shot dead."

After speculating on some of the circumstances that might lead to such a lethal encounter, I concluded the column by warning readers that:

> "...if you have any current plans to go to Florida, you might want to consider whether to pack a pistol along with the cabana wear, perhaps after first taking some time to master the art of the quick draw. After all, you never know when someone might take offense at something you say (even jokingly), decide to make their day at your expense, or simply perceive you as a threat requiring personal preemptive action. And in this case, forewarned might quite literally be forearmed."

Suffice it to say, more than eight years and some two dozen or so such state laws later—the dangers inherent in Florida's original "stand your ground" statute has suddenly become the focus of the U.S. attorney general and just about every news and public-affairs program being aired in the country, following the acquittal of former neighborhood watch volunteer George Zimmerman in the shooting death of unarmed black teenager Trayvon Martin. So much for the satisfaction of being able to say "I told you so" when (as I noted in a more recent column) "the thing that vindicates your views is some tragedy or calamity you could clearly see coming, yet with no power or influence to alter the course of events." Or, put another way, "for those of us who practice the art of punditry, there's only one thing worse than being proven wrong...and that's being proved right."

The following collection of "repeat offenders" is very much a mixed bag in terms of both tone and subject matter, ranging from the fanciful and satirical projections in the sections *Theories of Evolution* and *Trials and Errors*, to the somewhat more sober interpretations of worldly events offered in

REPEAT OFFENDERS

Observation Platforms. Some are intended to be slightly ridiculous (e.g., "Doing justice to the presidency"), while others readers may find somewhat revealing (e.g., the collusion between regulators and regulated suggested in the essay "Industry in the FDA's corner"), reflecting the fact a reporter's instinct is something one never quite loses. I trust those who read them, (or perhaps in some cases, re-read them), will be able to discern the difference.

I can only add in the unlikely event you still have a copy of a newspaper in which one of these first appeared (perhaps because you're a candidate for the TV show "Hoarders") and happen to notice slight variations in the current version, that's because I have taken the liberty of revising or re-editing each one as I saw fit—for as anyone in the business of writing will tell you, there are inevitably things that end up on the printed page that he or she would like to have done differently. You should also know whenever possible, I tried my best to avoid committing "unoriginal sin"—an offense repeated far too often these days by dateline-plagued pundits and reporters alike.

Bill Bonvie
Tuckerton, N.J.
July 2014
bonviebill@yahoo.com

* You won't find "Backword" in the dictionary so don't bother looking. It's a word I invented to mean the antithesis of "Foreword."

ILLUSION INTRUSIONS

A CAREER NEARLY NIPPED IN THE BUD BY AN ENCOUNTER WITH 'MR. QUAKER'

(Originally published in The Philadelphia Inquirer, April 2004, and featured at the Poynter Institute's Romenesko website.)

Like anyone who has toiled in the verbal vineyards of print journalism, I couldn't help but empathize with the plight of the two reporters whose recordings of a speech by U.S. Supreme Court Justice Antonin Scalia in Hattiesburg, Miss., were confiscated by a federal marshal.

I was particularly moved by how Antoinette Konz, a 25-year-old education reporter for the *Hattiesburg American*, described the experience to *New York Times* columnist Bob Herbert: "I went back to the office, and I just felt absolutely—I just felt horrible."

It reminded me of how I felt as a budding journalist during a long-ago encounter of my own, which, like Konz's, also took place at a high school assembly down South.

Unlike Konz, however, I was not yet a professional—and had I not been able to muster sufficient aplomb to rise above the psychological trauma and humiliation of the incident, I might never have become one. I was just beginning to learn the fundamentals of my craft on that day in 1961 at Winter Park High School in Florida when my journalism instructor assigned me to cover an appearance by a distinguished visitor—an iconic figure probably far more recognizable to us than Justice Scalia may have been to the students of Hattiesburg's Presbyterian Christian High School.

It was none other than "Mr. Quaker"—the real-life, authentically garbed symbol of the Quaker Oats Company, looking exactly as if he had just stepped off of a box of Puffed Rice.

Having no recording device, I went to the occasion prepared with a notepad and pen. Like the two reporters assigned to cover the good justice's speech, I ensconced myself in the front row of the auditorium so as not to miss a nugget of Mr. Quaker's wisdom.

And, just as they did, I soon discovered that calling attention to myself in that manner was a big mistake.

No sooner had I begun taking notes on Mr. Quaker's quotes than he paused and, fixing me with a glare made all the more stern by his austere attire, announced for all to hear that this was neither the time nor place to be doing one's homework.

Having thus been transformed in an instant from neophyte newsman into the cynosure of scorn, I self-consciously put aside my writing tools and, notwithstanding my sense of ignominy, tried as best as I could to mentally record the rhetorical points made by Mr. Quaker. From the account I ended up turning in (albeit one lacking in precise, accurate quotations), his sermon was very much in keeping with the ideas that many ideologues of that Cold War period were eager to instill in us.

In essence, he told us that the time was rapidly approaching when the Free World would have to confront the growing menace of communism, and that it was the members of our generation who would ultimately be called on to go out and meet it head on. Having conveyed that chilling (and somewhat prescient) message, Mr. Quaker climaxed his oratory with a dramatic recitation of Edward Everett Hale's "The Man Without a Country."

It was fortunate for me that, just as we were being dismissed, I was able to again catch Mr. Quaker's attention long enough to let him know what I was really doing there.

He was naturally very apologetic for having rebuked me so openly and for keeping me from carrying out my assignment in a more precise manner. At least I would not have to go around feeling forever upbraided by a glimpse of his white-locked countenance on supermarket shelves, in television commercials, or on the breakfast table.

What I failed to mention to him, however, was that I had spent a year attending a Quaker-run boarding school in Pennsylvania, and that his bellicose message somehow just didn't seem to jibe with the decidedly pacifistic views held by the Quakers of my acquaintance.

It would be a while before I developed enough nerve to raise that kind of discrepancy with the subject of a story or interview.

But my experience that day, I now realize, would prove more valuable to my career than most of the conventional lessons I learned in either my high school or college journalism classes. What it taught me was to always maintain a certain amount of skepticism toward the trappings of authority. For example, to no more expect a black-robed Supreme Court justice to embrace the First Amendment than to assume a costumed corporate faker personifies the quintessential Quaker.

And it taught me, whenever possible, to avoid front-row seats.

Author's note: The countenance of Mr. Quaker continues to grace boxes of Quaker Oats products, but he has more recently been referred to in advertising as "The Quaker Man." However, in March 2012, it was announced that his image was being given a makeover, with shorter hair, his double chin removed and "the rolls and plumpness in his face and neck" smoothed out to better exemplify the "energy and healthy choices" associated with oatmeal. (The news story on this change, incidentally, also gave his name as "Larry," which was definitely not the first name of the "Mr. Quaker" whose appearance I wrote about in high school.)

STARVING FOR ATTENTION

*(Originally published in The Berkshire Eagle and
The SandPaper, February 1996)*

Whenever any segment of the population is denied recognition, there's always the risk that its members might indulge in unseemly or even desperate acts to attain it.

A case in point is this country's sorry record of neglect and disdain toward one of its least visible and most misunderstood minority groups.

I'm talking, mind you, about human beings routinely being held back from self-actualization by a combination of inheritance and the prejudices peculiar to our society. As a result, they are often stripped of self-respect, frustrated in their aspirations and even deprived of the chance to pull themselves up by their bootstraps.

Indeed, the plight of America's affluent is nothing short of a national disgrace. To anyone with even an ounce of compassion, in fact, it should be obvious by now that, sequestered behind the walls of their elegant estates and penthouses, a good many of these "idle rich" are actually starving for attention.

That such appalling conditions need not exist has been amply demonstrated by other cultures that are more charitable and less mean-spirited toward those of means. In Britain, for instance, a simple title such as "Lord," "Lady," or "Sir" before one's name is usually sufficient to ensure that a wealthy person will be accorded a proper measure of esteem.

America, unfortunately, offers no such guarantees to individuals whom fortune has robbed of the right to otherwise distinguish themselves. Lacking any official acknowledgment of their nobility, such poor plutocratic souls have been too weighed down by wealth to rise to the challenge of daily survival so many others of us take for granted.

REPEAT OFFENDERS

Nor can they aspire to higher goals without having any potential accomplishment or position tainted in advance by suspicion of undue influence.

It's little wonder then, that the nation's well-heeled are having to resort to various indecorous—even bizarre—tactics in their determination to achieve some form of recognition.

A typical example is what American Express is currently offering to those crying-out-to-be-noticed members whose wealth permits them to accumulate 500,000 membership rewards—I'm talking about the once-in-a lifetime chance to be seen in a "fashion creation by Academy Award Winner Lizzy Gardiner."

Lizzy, the designer who, according to the company, "generated quite a charge" at last year's Oscar presentation with her "Gold Card Dress," is now described as ready to turn those half-a-million points into "your own outfit that people will be talking about for years." The offer includes a discussion with her of "your needs and ideas," your approval of sketches based on them, and, finally, the chance to make "a grand, conversation-stopping entrance" in the resulting getup.

The whole idea, then, seems to be one aimed at getting one's circle of friends and associates to stop talking about whatever topics they were discussing and talk about you instead (assuming, that is, that you're the person who can afford to charge the requisite amount of money on your American Express card).

To achieve that desired end, however, United Airlines may have come up with an even better idea.

According to its consumer bulletin, Friendly Skies, all an extremely frequent flier need do is submit the highest bid of 150,000 miles or more in the airline's frequent-flier-mile auction to "actually appear in a walk-on role" in an episode of the popular sitcom "Seinfeld" (with United providing the first-class transportation to boot).

Missing from this description is just what kind of walk-on role might be involved. Would a successful bidder be the object of Jerry's sarcasm, unthinkingly insulted by Elaine, used in some devious manner by George, perhaps even accidentally knocked out by Kramer? Or might he or she be the butt of some off-color or downright vulgar jest? It doesn't apparently matter—all that's really important is the importance that comes simply from making one's entrance on a top-rated show, being seen by millions, and becoming the resultant topic of discussion among one's social set.

Pathetic as they may appear, such promotions, which are no doubt the result of careful marketing research, represent the only real attempt to address the unfulfilled needs of America's elite—needs that can lead to ill-fated attempts at self-aggrandizement when society fails to take them seriously.

What better illustration of this can be given than one found on a 1987 postage stamp? The $5 stamp in question, according to a newspaper account, was issued by the Caribbean nation of Antigua and Barbuda, and bears the likeness of one John E. du Pont, identified as the "Father of Triathlon in the Americas" on the accompanying sheet, which depicts him running in "Team Foxcatcher" athletic garb along with portrayals of a cyclist and swimmer.

It also bears the name of a place called Redonda, an island that is essentially uninhabited. But that small deficiency didn't keep this particular heir to the du Pont fortune from reportedly paying $10,000 to be lionized by it on a stamp. So desperate was he for renown from any source.

No need to go into the rest of the sad saga of John E. du Pont, except to note that had he been living in a more enlightened and benevolent country, and accorded the honor of its stamp of approval and recognition—as "Lord Foxcatcher," say—instead of vainly attempting to create one, perhaps his subsequent descent into madness and murder could have been averted.

The point is that a little compassion in the form of a little recognition could go a long way toward helping those disadvantaged by excessive advantages. Remember, this is America –where being rich is something that can happen to anyone.

HOW AN ITSY-BITSY INCONGRUITY CAN UNRAVEL A 'GOSPEL TRUTH'

(Originally published in The SandPaper, November 2006)

As a veteran of the newspaper business, I've worn a variety of journalistic hats in the course of my somewhat haphazard career. In a couple of jobs, for instance, my headgear included that of people column editor on some nights and obituary page editor on others.

The people column could be fun, at least the way I liked to handle it, trying to come up with clever or humorous headlines and captions on various celebrity-related items. An example that comes to mind is a one-liner I devised for an interview with songwriter Randy Newman, in which he decried the fact that years after penning his song "Short People," he was still getting flak from those who failed to grasp that it was actually a parody on prejudice. "Short on comprehension" was the way I summed up that particular item.

The obituary page was something else entirely. In addition to being a far more solemn responsibility, it could be quite tedious, involving having to confirm numerous facts or fill in missing bits and pieces of information—at least the way I did it, which some of my colleagues thought was a little too picky. But I steadfastly maintained that accuracy and thoroughness were nowhere more important.

So it was with both interest and incredulity that I recently chanced to read an Associated Press obituary for Paul Van Valkenburgh of Ormond Beach, Florida, whose particular claim to fame was having written the 1960s pop hit "Itsy Bitsy Teenie Weenie Yellow Polka Dot Bikini" under the name Paul Vance.

What most intrigued me about this particular obit, however, was what it had to say about the military service record of Valkenburgh, whose age was given as 68. According to his wife, he was a Navy

REPEAT OFFENDERS

veteran of the Korean War—which, by my own calculations, would have made him no older than 15 at the time he allegedly served.

Perhaps he had lied about his age. But whatever the case, it was evident that someone at the AP had neglected to do their math homework before sending this story over the wires.

And sure enough, my suspicions that something was indeed amiss were confirmed a couple days later when I spotted a follow-up in, of all places, the people column. Only the misrepresentation involved turned out to be a lot more substantial than the discrepancy I had noticed.

It seems the late Mr. Valkenburgh had been merely pretending to be Paul Vance, who was actually alive and well and still receiving royalty payments for the song at his Coral Springs, Florida home.

Of course, had the writer of this off-base obituary (or the editor) taken the time to fact check the timeline of the Korean War (if he or she didn't already know it) and correlate it with the impostor's reported age, it might have given rise to other questions about its validity as well, and caused the entire fabric of this fabrication to unravel.

But the tendency to take things for granted and accept them at face value without even the most cursory examination seems to have become a component of our national character. We just assume that we're in possession of accurate information (once having assumed that it came from a reliable source)—then proceed on that assumption when, in fact, it may be a complete fallacy.

Think of all the faithful folks, for instance, who flocked to movie theaters a couple years ago to view the opus, *The Passion of the Christ*, not just for its agonizing reenactment for the Crucifixion, but on the apparent assumption that it somehow represented a repudiation of the much-despised Michael Moore's *Fahrenheit 9/11*.

This controversial—and rather gruesome—simulation, in fact, was constantly hyped by religious conservatives, including many right-wing clergy, as the cinematic antidote to the anti-Bush, anti-Iraq War venom contained in the Moore documentary.

Just why it became such an article of faith that Moore's tragicomic examination of the administration's response to the events of 9/11 was somehow contradicted by Mel Gibson's celluloid "Passion play" was never entirely clear. Perhaps it could be attributed to the belief that administration critics were just naturally "godless"—a holier-than-thou attitude on the part of many in the Bush camp that their born-again candidate's claim to divine guidance made any such attack on his policies equivalent to a crown of thorns, and its perpetrators in effect the anti-Christ.

Whatever the explanation, the idea that *The Passion* was the unofficial theme movie of the Bush campaign (as *Fahrenheit* seemed to be for its opposition) soon became one of those truths held by both the public and the media to be self-evident. Given such a popular presumption, the idea that the blue-collar radical Moore and the admittedly conservative Gibson might have shared similar sentiments would have been nothing short of heresy—so nobody apparently bothered to inquire.

It was therefore rather intriguing to read—again, in the people column, only two days before the bogus "bikini" obituary—that such was indeed the case.

It seems that while promoting his latest movie, *Apocalypto*, at a Texas film festival, Gibson couldn't resist comparing the present state of affairs with the collapse of the Mayan empire depicted in the film. "The precursors to a civilization that's going under are the same time and again," he said, adding, "What's human sacrifice if not sending guys off to Iraq for no reason?"

What I also found interesting was that this apparently cold sober assessment elicited nothing like the kind of furor with which the media and public responded to Gibson's drunken anti-Semitic harangue during a traffic stop. It didn't even come up during a much-hyped subsequent recent interview he had with ABC's Diane Sawyer, in which he attempted to reconcile his behavior while under the influence.

But then, Gibson himself had earlier acknowledged (also without a great deal of fanfare) that the idea he and Moore had made culturally and politically antithetical movies was in essence a hoax that had been perpetrated on the public. At the 31st Annual People's Choice awards back in January of last year, he admitted that he had seen *Fahrenheit* and "liked it," adding, "I feel a kind of strange kinship with Michael. I mean, they're trying to pit us against each other in the press,

REPEAT OFFENDERS

but…they've really got nothing to do with one another. They were used as some kind of divisive left-right thing." Moore, it should be noted, reciprocated by calling *Passion* a "powerful piece of filmmaking."

All of which, in retrospect, would appear to neatly jibe with what former White House insider David Kuo, describes as an administration that exploited the evangelical movement while privately deriding it in his newly released account, *Tempting Faith*.

And which, on a broader scale, should serve to once again remind us (as if the war itself wasn't enough) of the importance of critically examining the assumptions we're handed rather than simply accepting them as gospel truths.

It needn't take much, after all, to uncover the fact that we're being conned—perhaps no more than some itsy bitsy teenie weenie discrepancy buried in the back pages or the people column of your local paper—to start unraveling the whole thing. But by failing to do so, we can rest assured that we'll continue to be caught short on comprehension.

NOTES FROM THE ANTI-CONDOIST UNDERGROUND

(Originally published in the Hartford and Valley Advocates, 1987)

A community with a name like Greenacres City, Florida hardly sounds like the sort of place that could not accommodate a solitary gardenia.

Yet, that appears to be the case set forth in a $5,000 lawsuit filed against the Buttonwood Homeowners Association by a couple claiming that one of the association's officers deliberately ripped such a plant from their yard.

As if that wasn't bad enough, the plaintiffs allege that the association harassed them from the time they planted the gardenia in question and kept it under "surveillance."

Is it simply another one of those frivolous lawsuits? You might think so. But if you do, it's obvious that you've so far been spared the harsh realities of life under "Condoism."

As someone with first-hand knowledge of the tyrannies that this oppressive new system (which include so-called homeowners associations such as the aforementioned Buttonwood) is now spreading throughout the land, I can readily identify with the beleaguered plaintiffs in this matter.

Their experience, in fact, is reminiscent of one suffered by my own family a few years back, when a magnificent giant marigold that had been lovingly nurtured from a seedling beneath the window of our rented Connecticut condominium was unceremoniously cut down in the prime of life by one of the hired mercenaries who had become, in effect, a force of occupation (even while appearing to be occupied with a seemingly endless assortment of lawn and gardening tasks).

While the reported justification for the uprooting of the Greeacres City gardenia was that it stood in the way of mowers and sprinklers, no such excuse was even thought necessary for the extermination of our marigold. Its rationale, however, became evident enough only too soon in the form of a general communiqué from the head of the "garden committee" stressing said committee's intent to ensure that a "uniform" exterior appearance was maintained as strictly as possible.

No matter what the official explanation offered for such abuses, however, these and similar episodes represent what is often the first bold step to be taken by Condoist oppressors in the systematic subjugation of their neighbors: the abolition of fundamental floral freedom. In Condoist society, people soon learn that that cultivation of the bloom of their choice is something they must practice in secret deep within the interior recesses of their own units.

And that's only one of the numerous human-rights violations that routinely occur whenever Condoist governments successfully manage to usurp basic liberties.

Having lived in Condoist communities for several years as a "unit dweller" (more specifically, as a member of a subset of unit dwellers known as "renters," whom Condoist officials tend to regard as undesirables in their midst), and having spent much of that time as a clandestine member of the anti-Condoist underground, I can readily attest to the existence of many of these repressive practices in everyday life there, including:

Suppression of individualism. If there's anything that arouses the antipathy of a dedicated Condoist official, it's evidence of individualist tendencies among those existing within his or her domain. That's why Condoist governments will go to such unusual lengths to discourage activities reflecting individual initiative (e.g., the planting of nonconforming flowers) and to foster an image of "uniformity."

Unrelenting surveillance. Under Condoist rule, it isn't just something reserved for the likes of unauthorized gardenias. The chilling fact is that it's almost impossible to reside in a Condoist community without having the uncomfortable sensation that almost all of one activities and movements are under careful scrutiny—as indeed they are.

Nor are Condoist authorities content to limit such surveillance merely to exteriors, where routine patrols are ever on the alert for rule violations, such as outlawed decorative objects and recreational equipment on unit balconies and patios deemed part of the "common area." Indeed, there have been instances of people being spied on inside the supposed privacy of their bedrooms—again by these same ubiquitous grounds keepers, whom residents have spotted standing just outside their windows by the dawn's early light.

Stifling of dissent. Like authoritarian regimes everywhere, the "boards" and "associations" that rule condominium collectives have little tolerance for anyone who dares to openly voice opposition to their policies or pronouncements. The most common measure employed to silence such dissenters is the threat of fines. Ostensibly intended to curb proscribed behavior and rule infractions, such fines in actuality represent a convenient means of cracking down on suspected subversives.

Served on targeted individuals without any semblance of due process, notices of fines are usually accompanied or followed by threats of liens and confiscation of property if said penalties are not promptly paid and supposed violations immediately desisted from. In the case of renters, fines may be used to apply pressure to landlords to have the offending unit dweller driven into permanent exile from the community.

An episode that recently occurred in a typical suburban condo complex provides a chilling illustration of the manner in which such measures are routinely utilized for purposes of intimidation and coercion. It involved a usually mild-mannered former reporter who had just ventured out of his rented condo unit for the purpose of taking the family dog for a midday walk (the canine in question, a valued toy poodle, always being scrupulously leashed when outdoors). Hearing shouts behind him, accompanied by a loud cracking noise, he turned around just in time to see a large tree come crashing to earth at a point both he and the dog had traversed only seconds before. The fallen sycamore had landed not only squarely across the sidewalk, but the street as well, thus blocking the only vehicular access to and egress from the complex itself.

Ascertaining that this close call had not been due to an act of god, but rather to that of a tree-cutting service, the ex-reporter politely attempted to make known his concern about the incident to the foreman, only to find himself rebuffed in the most unpleasant terms imaginable. Somewhat put off by this response, the near-victim spotted the individual in charge of performing maintenance duties, whom he proceeded to apprise of the incident. The maintenance supervisor replied that he, too, had had occasion to observe the carelessness of these particular tree cutters, and asked if the indignant renter would mind accompanying him to the upcoming "Board" meeting to relate what had occurred to those responsible for engaging their services.

Thus reinforced, the chagrined ex-reporter ventured the following night into the presence of the Board— a more forbidding and stern-visaged panel than ever he recalled having encountered in all his years of covering various governmental bodies—and, after providing his name and unit number, proceeded to give an account of what had taken place. Other than a perfunctory thank you, however, he received no immediate reply. He did, however, chance to bump into the maintenance supervisor the next day, only to learn that the latter had just been summarily relieved of his duties.

It took a bit longer for an official response of sorts to arrive from an officer of the Board, which while it made no direct reference to the tree-cutting complaint, did have a lot to say on the subject of "dog roaming." According to the official, the unit dwellers residing at the renter's address had been warned about dog roaming "many times." Accompanying the notice was a rather unpleasant ultimatum from the renter's corporate landlord.

Torture. The notion that, amid the apparent suburban tranquility of such an enlightened country as ours, people are actually being tortured may be an extremely difficult one for many Americans to accept. I might have had difficulty believing it myself were it not for my own personal knowledge of the fact that deep inside the confines of Condoist enclaves, specialists in the art of torture are routinely engaged to indiscriminately inflict it on men, women and children of all ages.

The method of torture most favored is the use of giant lawn-mowers, multiple leaf blowers and other electrically powered gardening devices whose decibel emissions can be amplified to excruciatingly painful levels for unbearably long periods of time. (It is especially apt to be employed whenever a unit dweller attempts to communicate with the outside world via long-distance telephone.)

Chemical warfare. The easiest way to maintain tight control of a resident population, Condoist officials have found, is to make sure they congregate only inside easily monitored enclosures such as swimming pools and clubhouses (the units themselves not being generally designed to accommodate gatherings of any size). They've therefore devised a terrifyingly effective technique for preventing outdoor gatherings during periods of ideal weather.

The tactic involves the deployment of teams of mercenaries armed with evil-looking devices and nozzles whose sole purpose is to disseminate toxic chemicals throughout the immediate environment. Caught off guard, I have witnessed panic-stricken mothers grab their baby carriages and make a frantic dash for safety before these fearful onslaughts of poison, the noxious fumes from which often linger in the atmosphere for days afterward.

Of course, the "official" explanation given for these shocking violations of civilized standards of decency are always the same: they are merely harmless strategies intended to defend lawns and shrubs against various undesirable insects and weeds.

With more and more families and retirees gravitating towards condominium communities in the mistaken belief that all they are surrendering is the burden of performing their own maintenance chores, the growing menace of Condoism is finding increasingly fertile ground in which to thrive and threaten the very foundations of our liberty. And should you be the least bit skeptical about the tyranny posed by this particular threat, just remember: every cherished freedom we consider to be part of our birthright as Americans, is to the Condoist mentality merely another gardenia standing in the way of mowers and sprinklers.

Author's note: In the years since this piece appeared, a far greater number of Americans have fallen under the domination of Condoism, which remains as repressive and unrepentant as ever.

MAKING A MONKEY BUSINESS CONNECTION

(Originally published in The SandPaper, May 2006)

Sometimes, you may think you know someone really well, only to wake up one morning and find out that they've been keeping an important part of their identity hidden from you.

Take my sister Linda, for example. She's probably the last person I'd ever have suspected of being a Republican. That's not just because she voted for the Democratic ticket in the last presidential election (or so I thought), but because I've never known her to be either involved in politics or to identify with typical GOP concerns.

So you can well imagine my surprise upon learning that she's actually among New Jersey's top Republican business leaders.

It was only because I chanced to take a phone call intended for her one morning last week while she was out walking the dog, in fact, that I became privy to this somewhat startling revelation, along with the news that she was being offered an honorary chairmanship of the National Republican Congressional Committee's Business Advisory Council. In keeping with this esteemed position, she would be regularly invited to attend dinner meetings with important decision makers in Washington, including President Bush himself, to help them in "cutting taxes and moving the president's small business agenda forward."

Even though all this may have come as something of a shock, I must admit I was quite impressed. So much so, in fact, that I may even have given the caller the impression I was Linda—not because I was attempting to arrogate her accolades, you understand, but simply because I was at that moment overwhelmed by curiosity (keeping in mind that any unwitting deception in which I may have engaged is probably due to the subliminal influence of people like Karl Rove and other key Republican figures of the past few years).

Naturally, the first thing I endeavored to ascertain was how she'd

REPEAT OFFENDERS

been chosen for such a distinction. While my caller was a bit vague on this point, I was able to gather that both "achievements" and "public records" figured significantly in the selection process.

Might there have been any connection, I wondered, to "Chunky Monkey LLC"?

That's the name of a small business Linda recently registered under the "toys and games" classification to serve as a marketing venue for the original Chunky Monkey doll and related intellectual property that we had inherited from our mom, cartoonist Pauline Comanor. Nowhere that I know of, however, was any reference ever made in the filing (or on the chunkymonkey.com website) to Chunky Monkey's being a political-party animal, let alone a Republican primate.

But before I could explore this any further with the person on the line, she switched me over to a short audio tape made by the head of the NRCC, Congressman Tom Reynolds (R-N.Y.), who talked a bit about how the government should be helping to free small businesses from the burden of oppressive taxes—an apparent goal of the Business Advisory Council. Once that message had concluded, a second person took over the call (which the woman to whom I originally spoke may admittedly have found a bit challenging).

After praising the worthiness of the objective cited on the tape by Rep. Reynolds, I remarked as to how I would certainly welcome a chance to have dinner with President Bush, having long hoped for the opportunity to ask him whether spending hundreds of billions of dollars on the war he chose to wage in Iraq might, in fact, not actually be inflating our oppressive tax burden. A good point, she replied, but we had to help the Iraqis with their democracy, too.

Then, apparently not the least bit put off by either my questioning of presidential priorities or by my unawareness of any Republican party affiliation on Linda's part, she went on to ask whether her name could be added to the list of state chairmen to be featured in a full-page ad the NRCC was planning to run in *The Wall Street Journal* as a way of according formal recognition to its Business Advisory Council.

By this time, however, the real Linda had returned from her walk, so I handed the phone over to her with a brief explanation. She proceeded to uncercmoniously reject the offer of the honorary state chairmanship, along with the presidential dinner invitation, her name on the *Journal* ad, and the honorary gavel that is provided to each honorary chairman, as depicted on the Business Advisory Council's website. (In so doing, according to the same site, she also turned down the chance to participate in periodic strategy sessions and to help provide "the seed money needed to create the grassroots support that can finally lead to a breakthrough on health care reform, debt reduction, social security, tax and education reform, and sound economic policy that keeps this economy growing!")

I might have let the matter rest there, had I not had a nagging curiosity to find out what had prompted the NRCC to offer my sister this less-than-singular honor in the first place. So I started making some phone calls of my own, starting with the NRCC itself.

After acknowledging, "we probably made an error in assuming that she's a Republican at all," the representative with whom I spoke—a chap named Hank—also admitted he was at something of a loss to tell me exactly what the selection process entailed. He did suggest I talk to an executive of an Akron, Ohio-based organization called InfoCision, which is responsible for making the actual calls, and which bills itself as "THE highest quality call center company in the world."

I called InfoCision, only to be told the individual Hank suggested I confer with was out of town. The woman who assisted him, however, was of the opinion that to be considered for an honorary chairmanship, it would be necessary to have "shown some sort of interest in the Republican party"—perhaps via a conservative website. She then offered to have someone with more knowledge of the process call me back.

When a couple of days had passed and no one did, I once again took it upon myself to call InfoCision. It was almost closing time on Friday, but this time, I struck pay dirt by getting through to an account representative named John Zawaski. "We get lists of business owners throughout the country," was how he explained it. The company then evaluates such factors as the type of industry, the number of employees, and its sales volume, as well as looking at executive titles. "If they're an executive or a CEO, typically, those would be the people we contact.

REPEAT OFFENDERS

"What we're doing is we're prospecting for people who want to join our business council," he added. "Typically, we've found from our research that certain business owners in certain industries tend to be Republicans."

So there was the answer to my query: you need not be active in Republican business circles in order to be selected as an honorary chairman of the Business Advisory Council of the National Republican Congressional Committee. It only matters that you appear to fit the profile of an entrepreneur whose particular type of endeavor has what might be regarded as a Republican-sounding ring to it.

And who would seem a more likely candidate for a red-carpet reception into Republican Party ranks than someone who's openly engaged in monkey business?

CHRISTMAS: THE WHOLE SCHMEAR

(Originally published in The Philadelphia Inquirer, December 2007)

About four decades ago, a comedy album called *Have a Jewish Christmas...?* offered a hilarious take on what it might be like if typical American Jews were to abandon their constraints on engaging in traditional Yuletide festivities.

We sure could use an album of that caliber today. Its depictions of things like two Jewish neighbors trying to outdo each other in outdoor decor, elderly Tanta Sophie reacting to seeing "Jewish people with Goyish trees" by remarking, "If mine husband would be alive, he would die," and nocturnal visits from the "Hanukkah ghost," might provide us with some welcome relief from Americans' increasingly uptight attitudes toward their "beliefs."

In fact, it's my belief that in most cases, such "beliefs" aren't really true beliefs in the sense of well-reasoned convictions, but rather unquestioned ideas associated with customs and traditions imbued in our psyches during childhood.

But should you believe that all Jews are compelled by their beliefs to spend December 25th in a self-imposed Chinese-restaurant exile, I'm here to tell you otherwise. There are those who are every bit as proficient as any gentile when it comes to decking the halls. I should know, because I'm one of them.

Yes, I do the whole schmear: the tree, the cards, the last minute shopping, the caroling, the jing-a-linging, and the general jollifying.

Of course, considering my last name, you may suspect that my enthusiastic embrace of the occasion is due to having a non-Jewish parent. While it's true my stepfather introduced a Christmas tree to our household, it only served to complement a celebration that was already a well-entrenched family tradition.

For that, I can really thank my maternal grandparents, Harry and

REPEAT OFFENDERS

Fanny Comanor, who were moved by the Christmas spirit after arriving here from Russia about a century ago, as was a contemporary Russian Jewish compatriot of theirs named Israel Isidore Baline (to whom I shall return in just a moment).

But it isn't merely tradition that compels me to revel in this ritual every year. I'm also drawn to its nostalgic and aesthetic aspects—its ability to evoke some of my fondest childhood memories. A menorah, notwithstanding its symbolic significance, is simply no match for an artistically decorated, colorfully lit Christmas tree when it comes to brightening up and beautifying one's environment.

Likewise, I'm perennially enchanted by the season's magnificent music, and even play some of it on my beat-up guitar (although admittedly that Brooklyn-born Jewish bard, Neil Diamond, does a much better job). Should singing carols be reserved for true believers in the biblical account of the birth of the baby Jesus? Come now: Does singing "Santa Claus Is Coming to Town" require a literal belief in the lyrics?

Then there's the view (supported by my dictionary) of the occasion as a stupendous secular festival to which no invitation is needed. I, therefore, see no reason not to attend, especially since it's ostensibly meant to honor a member of my own tribe (whether or not one chooses to believe he was a divinity).

To those who might feel affronted by such sentiments, I can only ask whether they take similar umbrage upon hearing that most popular of all songs, "White Christmas," which was written by the aforementioned Israel Isidore Baline after he disembarked on these shores and changed his name to Irving Berlin.

Still, most Jews would not feel comfortable joining in the festivities—even if they'd secretly love to (as I have no doubt many would). But Christmas is essentially an international holiday, an occasion of good cheer that people of all faiths (including those of little or no faith) are free to celebrate, if they so choose. Whether it's considered a holy day as well should also be purely a matter of individual choice.

So, to paraphrase a line from a famous editorial: Yes, Virginia, there is indeed such a thing as a Jewish Christmas.

Author's note: This article undoubtedly rates as the all-time biggest "offender" of any of those included in this collection. As the editor of the page noted in introducing a whole group of letters entirely devoted to it: "Bill Bonvie's Dec. 24 commentary, "Christmas: the whole schmear," about being Jewish and celebrating Christmas, brought strong reactions from readers." What follows are a few samples of those responses (which, incidentally, all came from members of 'the Tribe'):

"While I understand Bonvie's lament that a Christmas tree is more fun than a menorah, I believe that borrowing another's holiday without regard for its religious significance is disrespectful to those who fully observe that holiday. Furthermore, it is our job as Jewish parents to instill delight in our children for our customs, and build rituals and memories around them."

"To suggest that there is such a thing as a 'Jewish Christmas' is an insult to Christians everywhere, and a slap in the face to American Jews who struggle every day with their identities."

"'Oy vey'" is what I say to Bill Bonvie."

(All of which is further evidence of what I said at the beginning of this piece about needing relief from "Americans' increasingly uptight attitudes towards their 'beliefs'"—and that saying anything that might challenge those beliefs is still the most sure-fire way to give offense.)

ELEVATING THE 'NANNY STATE' TO SUPERNANNY NATION STATUS

(Originally published in The SandPaper, July 2008)

If there's anything that tends to rankle red-blooded Americans, it's the idea of being told what not to do by a so-called "nanny state."

Such resentment, in fact, was the subject of a book published just last year, "Nanny State," by conservative *Denver Post* columnist David Harsanyi, in which the author chronicles what, in his view, are numerous examples of meddlers, moralists, politicians, and "boneheaded bureaucrats" turning America into "a nation of children."

While some may consider that assessment to be a bit overblown, its applicability to one governmental entity in particular would be hard to deny. For the fact remains that when it comes to treating us all like a throng of ten-year-olds, there's nothing that can begin to match the authoritarian approach of the Bush Administration.

Remember, for instance, how back when you were a kid, any discussion of certain subjects was apt to be taboo? In similar fashion, the Decider and his deputies have determined that there are things in this world that you're simply better off not knowing about—even if you're now considered mature enough to attend an R-rated movie without being escorted by a parent or guardian.

One such delicate matter is that of the world's changing climate.

It seems that an Environmental Protection Agency assessment that global warming could pose a danger to the public, made last December in the form of a 28-page report, was just not considered suitable for said public to peruse. And when members of Congress conducting a hearing on the role the White House played in EPA decision-making attempted to find out the reason from EPA Administrator Stephen Johnson, he simply declined to tell them, causing the hearing to be canceled.

REPEAT OFFENDERS

This may be a bit reminiscent of how your mother or father (or nanny, if they could afford one) might have responded to a similar question from you: "Because I said so, that's why."

But if you must have some inkling of a possible reason why the White House Budget Office would even refuse to open an e-mail containing the report, it may have something to do with the fact that last year, the Supreme Court ruled that any such conclusion would compel the EPA to regulate emissions of greenhouse gases from motor vehicles. And that, in turn, might have ending up causing you additional expense and inconvenience.

So, you see, it was quite likely for your own good that you and your fellow Americans were denied permission to view the report in question.

But that, as it turns out, isn't the only thing those in charge of the EPA would rather you not read.

A couple years ago, for instance, it was decided that all the data on pesticides and other toxic chemicals contained in the agency's research libraries should henceforth be off limits—not only to the public, but to the EPA's own scientists as well. (Supposedly, it would all eventually be "digitized" at some undisclosed time—which is a bit like what I was told by a librarian upon requesting a certain book at the age of 12: "When you get older.")

This, naturally, didn't sit well with some of the researchers who used those facilities, and would now have to rely on the chemical industry for their information. They took their complaints to Congress, which agreed that perhaps the administration had gone a bit overboard in protecting them, and ordered the libraries reopened. But so far, only a fraction of what they contained has been made available, and in much smaller and less accessible quarters than before.

There has, however, been one new feature added—an official library overseer, whose responsibilities will include supervising all research and information requests and deciding what material ought to be dispensed with.

Then there was the recent report in *The Washington Post* of an attempt by political appointees at the Department of Labor to sneak in a new rule making it more difficult to regulate workers' exposures to chemicals and toxins. According to the paper's account, the agency ignored a requirement that it disclose the plan in public notices filed in December and May, opting instead to publish it on the Office of Management and Budget's website in July using only a nine-word title.

Such goings-on can't help but call to mind the way our parents might have tried to keep certain topics from corrupting our childish innocence by postponing any discussion of them until after our bedtime—and then using only "code words" in case we might be eavesdropping at the top of the stairs.

At times, the administration's tendency to overprotect Americans, including government employees, might even remind us of how we were sometimes forbidden to see a particular movie, or to accompany a playmate on a visit to a certain unapproved locale or event.

An example was last week's huge public rally for presumptive Democratic Presidential nominee Barack Obama in Berlin, Germany, which U.S. State Department officials were given strict orders not to attend by Ambassador Robert Timken (an Ohio businessman who just happens to be a good buddy of President Bush).

According to another *Washington Post* article, the mandate was formulated by State Department Undersecretary for Management Patrick F. Kennedy, who said it was intended to ensure that foreign service officials remained unsullied by exposure to a "partisan political act." (And while this edict may have struck the American Foreign Service Association as a wee bit excessive, its 11th-hour timing reportedly rendered the group's opposition moot.)

Considering such constraints on the conduct of the citizenry, the Bush Administration's enlisting the help of telecommunications companies to monitor our phone calls and e-mail—and even claiming the right to open our regular mail when it sees fit—becomes simply another manifestation of a much larger parental pattern.

That's why, when history stands in judgment of this regime's most notable achievements—a manufactured war, the arbitrary suspension of habeas corpus, the authorization of torture, the abduction of individuals to Third-World prisons, and the routine use of "signing statements" as a way of disregarding various provisions of new laws—I have no doubt that what is perhaps its greatest domestic contribution will be included in the assessment.

In essence, we must never be allowed to forget how this president and his associates have succeeded in expanding the traditional notion of a "nanny state" into the creation of an actual Supernanny Nation.

INDUSTRY IN THE FDA'S CORNER

(Originally published in The SandPaper, February 2011)

Regulation, or so goes the political rhetoric from some folks on the right, is anathema to industry. Cutting regulatory agencies down to size has thus become a primary objective of the smaller-government crowd that was voted into partial power in November, based on its belief that less oversight will give corporations more room to spread their wings.

The only problem with this idea is that a sizable part of the corporate sector itself seems to have embraced just the opposite philosophy, and is actually calling for a beefed-up regulatory presence.

You say you weren't aware of that? Well, quite frankly, neither was I until just the other day, when in the process of doing an Internet search for some unrelated piece of information, I chanced to stumble on the Web site of the "Alliance for a Stronger FDA."

This particular organization, created in 2006, based in Washington, D.C., and whose web address is www.strengthenFDA.org, purports to have two stated goals: to assure that the U.S. Food and Drug Administration has sufficient resources to protect patients and consumers, and to maintain public confidence and trust in the FDA.

It also claims an impressive membership list, which includes seven former FDA commissioners, three former secretaries of the U.S. Department of Health and Human Services, some 86 nonprofit groups (mostly health-and-wellness-related), another 24 trade associations, 23 companies, and 14 law and consulting firms, as well as some 30 individual members.

But what I found really interesting was the identities of the trade associations and companies who are in favor of strengthening the FDA. The former run the gamut of industries falling under the purview of that agency, from the American Frozen Food Institute and the Grocery

Manufacturers Association to the Society of the Plastics Industry and the Personal Care Products Institute. As for the latter, they read almost entirely like a Who's Who of the pharmaceutical industry (whose trade association is also on board, along with those of FDA-regulated medical manufacturing devices).

Curious as to why all these concerns would be so concerned about government regulators not having enough resources to adequately regulate them, I thought I'd pursue the question with one of its media contacts, and ended up having a pleasant and informative chat with Steve Grossman, the group's deputy executive director.

"All FDA stakeholders want a strong, consistent, predictable deadline-meeting FDA," explained Grossman, whose background includes having served as deputy assistant secretary for health under the Reagan Administration. "Everybody who is overseen by the FDA benefits when the agency is seen as strong and competent and a gold standard for the world."

While Grossman acknowledged that "on any given day, every one of these companies has a complaint about something the FDA is doing," still "they understand that their concerns won't be made better by the agency's having fewer resources," including staff. One reason, he noted, is that a regulatory body that lacks people qualified to "investigate the science and run the lab tests" is prone to "make the most conservative decisions because it doesn't want to do anything wrong." Another is that U.S. industries export a lot of products, which makes it especially important to have a "strong FDA that's recognized worldwide as being a leader in science and regulation."

So that, in a nutshell, is why some of the biggest names in the business of making things that consumers quite literally consume have allied themselves with (and even paid dues toward) the efforts of this "advocacy and educational organization" to make sure the FDA gets its fair share of the fiscal pie.

Just this month, for example, the group "responded with concern" to the House Appropriations Committee's announcement of proposed cuts in the agency's funding, with its president, Nancy Bradish Myers (who's also president of Catalyst Healthcare Consulting) noting in a press release that "We certainly understand the need to reduce the federal budget, but want to be sure that Congress has a clear picture of how FDA contributes to economic growth and national security, as well as protecting our public health."

But just how good a job does—or can—the FDA do of "protecting public health" when some of its top officials have themselves had prior affiliations with the industries it regulates? The current FDA commissioner, Margaret Hamburg, to cite just one example, participated in rule making on dental amalgams, which contain toxic mercury, after having served as director of Henry Schein Inc., the largest seller of amalgams.

Then there's the case of Michael Taylor, who was named a year ago as the agency's deputy commissioner for foods. Taylor, who was listed as a guest speaker at an Alliance membership meeting only last week and also met with the group last summer, used to be vice president for public policy at Monsanto, a position that merits only a cursory mention in the last sentence of the FDA's announcement of his appointment.

Now Monsanto, as you may be aware, is the biotech giant that produces the genetically modified (or GM) seeds that now account for most of the nation's soy, canola, field corn and cotton having become genetically modified crops, with the stage now set for alfalfa and sugar beets to go the same route. This has been an economic boon to the company both through its control of the seed market and in the fact that the main purpose of such bioengineered crops is to make them "Roundup Ready"—that is, able to withstand the effects of Monsanto's glyphosate herbicide Roundup.

However, the technology involved—which is also one of our exports—has been strongly opposed by environmentalists, who point out that its safety was never established and that what tests have been performed on such "Frankenfoods" don't bode well for consumers. And that's not to mention the extensive use of glyphosate, which has also been quite controversial. But the reason the government has never performed safety testing on GM crops is that back in 1992 the FDA ruled it wasn't needed—a policy that Taylor reportedly had a lead role in formulating while in a previous FDA post following an earlier stint at Monsanto. And while Monsanto is not listed as an Alliance member, the Biotechnology Industry Organization to which it belongs is.

So I put the 'revolving door' question directly to Grossman, who responded that the Alliance is narrowly focused on making sure the FDA isn't starved for funds and does not involve itself in staffing issues.

The Alliance's membership roster, however, was a source of some concern to Jim Turner, a long-time Washington, D.C. consumer advocate lawyer and author of "The Chemical Feast," the Nader Study Group report on food protection and the FDA, whom I contacted after speaking with Grossman. "It always makes me nervous," he responded, "when I see a private organization with influential former government officials as members working together with regulated companies to 'strengthen' the power of the regulating agency that controls their marketing rules."

Perhaps you find that a bit unsettling as well. Or then again, maybe you're among those who firmly believe that the less oversight capability a bureaucracy like the FDA possesses, the better it is for business. But before you accept that premise as a given, perhaps you really ought to find out if the particular business you have in mind concurs. You might be surprised to find the business is more inclined to think that to 'starve the regulatory beast' would be akin to killing the goose that lays the "gold standard" egg for American industry.

Author's note: Nearly a year after this article was published, a petition was circulated by MoveOn.org protesting President Obama's appointment of Michael Taylor as senior adviser to the commissioner of the FDA, which characterized allowing Monsanto "to have free rein in U.S. food policy" as "a nightmare scenario that is against the interest of all Americans and world citizens."

THEORIES OF EVOLUTION

TAKING CREDIT FOR AN IDEA THAT FLEW (AND COULD FLY A WHOLE LOT HIGHER)

(Originally published in The SandPaper, November 2007)

Ideas are funny things. There are occasions when they can hit you from out of the blue, and other times when they might be inspired by some item you read or hear about in the news.

An example of the latter is the idea I got for this column, which came to me after reading in *The Press of Atlantic City* about the two retired ad agency employees who were squabbling over which of them came up with the idea for the slogan, "Please don't squeeze the Charmin."

The dispute followed the death of Dick Wilson, the actor who played the part of Mr. Whipple, the grocery-store clerk identified with the famous line in TV commercials. It began after Norman Schaut of Ocean City said the phrase came to him while preparing a store display for the Madison Avenue firm of Benton & Bowles back in 1964.

No sooner had he made that claim, however, when John Chervokas of Ossining, N.Y., came forth to say that the line had, in fact, been his original creation while working at the same agency, and that he had never even heard of Shaut until the story came to his attention.

As it turned out, neither of the conflicting claims could be confirmed at this late date, with the managing editor of *Advertising Age* being quoted as observing how such feuds over who did what are all too common in a business where individuals are seldom credited for their creative efforts.

Having spent a sizable chunk of my own career in the ad biz, I can second that. In fact, it reminded me to some degree of the line—actually, a couple of lines—that I penned (yes, literally using a pen) back in 1983 while working as a copywriter at a medium-size, family-owned ad agency located in a suburb of Hartford, Connecticut.

On that particular morning, the agency's entire creative staff had been ordered to attend a meeting that had been hastily convened in the conference room with a team of idea people (or so we were led to believe) from Pratt & Whitney, the giant aircraft-engine manufacturer whose plant was a few miles away.

As they explained it, the company was initiating an employee suggestion program, with cash bonuses, as well as personal recognition, to be awarded for any ideas that could save the company money or make its operations more efficient. Our job, which was to take priority over everything else we were doing at the moment, was to try to come up with an attention-getting name for this program.

Returning to my office following this momentous meeting, I took up a pen and yellow legal pad and briefly pondered the challenge at hand. In order to win this little competition, clearly I would have to come up with the kind of idea that would fly with both the agency brass and the Pratt & Whitney people…just like the ideas the program was aimed at eliciting. So there it was, my first idea, which I jotted down within about a minute or two of leaving the meeting: "Ideas That Fly," which just happened to have the added advantage of having a perfect tie-in with the company's products.

But I couldn't come to my superiors with just one idea, so in the next half hour or so, I came up with several more, which were somewhat less memorable, as I've now forgotten what they were. I then turned in my list, the two other copywriters submitted theirs, and we waited to see whose, if anyone's, ideas might fly.

As it turned out, we didn't have to wait long. Within a couple of days, the entire art department was busy designing prospective logos to go along with…"Ideas that Fly," one of which—a depiction of a jet taking off from what appeared to be a runway of yellow bars on a blue background—ultimately flew.

Somewhere during this agency-shaking process, it fell on me to create an accompanying slogan to be used primarily on "Ideas That Fly" cafeteria cards at the behemoth P&W plant. It didn't take long for one to hit me from out of the blue: "They can hit you from out of the blue."

But other than that indirect acknowledgment, I can't say I recall anyone giving me any particular recognition for coming up with the "big idea" in the form of, say, a bonus or even being taken out to lunch. I did, however, get taken to lunch a few months later by the new creative director who had been hired away from another agency, and who used the occasion to ask me why I was no longer as dedicated as I had been when I first came aboard, as indicated by the fact I was no longer staying late without getting paid any overtime. I didn't bother telling him that copywriting, unlike journalism, my other profession, was something I did strictly for the money.

The only comment I can recall being made to me, in fact, was from one of my copywriter colleagues. "I remember seeing that idea," she said. "But I didn't think it sounded high-tech enough."

But that was how it was with the ad biz, with individual creative achievements invariably being assimilated into the "team effort" and the agency itself ultimately taking the credit.

I have no idea, in fact, whether anyone else involved ever claimed to have created "Ideas That Fly" (and you'll simply have to take my word for it that I was its originator).

Not so the "Ideas That Fly" program itself, however, for which various P&W employees were accorded both accolades and monetary rewards. I know, because I still have a copy of the photo that appeared in *The Hartford Courant* showing a smiling worker named Rhonda Pease, framed by an American flag and a large poster featuring the "Ideas That Fly" title and logo along with the words "the New P&W Suggestion Program." She had just gotten an $8,500 award from the company for an idea that, in addition to simplifying her job, was reported to have saved her bosses a cool million that year.

And that brings me around to the idea that came to me for this column—not just for this column, actually, but for the entire country.

Most of us, I think, would readily acknowledge that America and its economy are in a pretty messed up state these days. And there are undoubtedly many private citizens out there with enough expertise, experience or just plain horse sense to provide workable ideas that could both make things run more efficiently and probably save taxpayers billions—but who currently have no viable vehicle available for conveying such proposals to the proper government agencies.

REPEAT OFFENDERS

What I therefore would like to propose is an official nationwide suggestion program along the lines of "Ideas That Fly," complete with financial incentives and awards ceremonies. The prospect of being accorded both personal recognition and some extra bucks to boot, I feel reasonably certain, would be sufficient to spur such ingenious individuals to cultivate and submit ideas for streamlining government and perhaps even improving the lives of Americans in the process.

Moreover, once those ideas deemed most innovative were given prominent play in the media, it would be a lot harder for government to simply disregard or shelve them and go on with the business of wastefulness and inefficiency as usual.

Now there's just one thing such a program would need—a clever, enticing title. And, no doubt, you think I've got a bunch of them in mind. But even if I did, or could come up with a likely winner in a minute, I wouldn't offer it in a context such as this.

That's because once you've been in the ad biz, you can't help but be aware of how high a price clients are willing to pay for ideas of that sort. And the idea of getting recompensed for an idea is a far better incentive than the idea of simply getting recognized as its creator.

Author's note: In the spring of 2013, I got a message via LinkedIn from Frank Sorano, who worked as a graphic artist at the above-mentioned ad agency and whom I had not seen or spoken with in nearly 30 years. When I asked Frank (who still lived in Connecticut) if he was the one who conceived the "Ideas That Fly" logo, he said it would be OK to mention him in this context as part of the four-person "team" that designed it. Such veracity is a refreshing contrast to the way certain noncreative players in the ad biz are all too ready to take credit for other people's work.

A BRAVE NEW WORLD OF PHARMACOLOGICAL POSSIBILITIES

(Originally published in The Berkshire Eagle and The San Francisco Chronicle, February 1989)

Anyone who fears that our nation may be losing its nerve should be considerably heartened by the recent disclosure of a plan to chemically preserve America's long-held reputation as the home of the brave.

Believe it or not (depending on the amount of credibility you attach to a television network news report that appears to have otherwise received scant media attention), work is now underway on a "brave pill" in the research labs of Walter Reed Army Medical Center.

This possible harbinger of our very own "brave new world" would supposedly provide American soldiers in future conflicts with a "chemical suit of armor" designed to boost their courage by reducing their physiological reactions to the stresses of combat, according to the report.

While the idea of awarding medals based on medication may be the subject of some initial controversy, its eventual acceptance in military circles is probably inevitable (especially if our enemies start developing something along the same lines). At that point, it's only natural that civilian pharmaceutical firms will begin to express an interest, ultimately leading to the day when courage becomes an over-the-counter commodity readily available from your local druggist and pitched by Madison Avenue in the all-too-familiar manner:

Attractive single gal: I had a survival instinct this big—and it was keeping me from participating in so many enjoyable activities, like mountain climbing, sunbathing and casual sex. Life just wasn't any fun any more. Then a friend introduced me to VALORIUM.

REPEAT OFFENDERS

Announcer: With new maximum-strength VALORIUM, you get the benefit of not just one, but three battlefield-tested ingredients guaranteed to take the worry out of taking risks.

Attractive single gal (climbing Mount Everest): I had a survival instinct this big…but now it's gone. And thanks to VALORIUM, I couldn't care less if the same thing happens to me.

Before long, encouraged by the growing consumer demand for such products, pharmaceutical houses will become engaged in a high-powered competition to develop entire new lines of drugs aimed at promoting other attributes as well. And television viewers will find themselves being blitzed with such messages as:

(Scene: Oxford University campus)
Announcer: When 1,000 doctoral candidates were asked what they'd most prefer to have along if enrolled in a place like this, more than 70 percent chose ACUMEN over such intelligence boosters as IQ and COMPREHEND. ACUMEN…the smart way to make yourself appear a whole lot smarter.

Or:

Executive #1: Can't we postpone this meeting until some other time? (Yawns) I'm just not myself today.
Executive #2: You have been looking kind of tired, Phil. Having any trouble sleeping?
Executive #1: To tell the truth, I've been having a lot of trouble sleeping lately. In all the years Myrna and I have been married, I've never once cheated on her…that is, until this month when I started having an affair with my secretary. Now I'm tormented by this nagging guilt, and it's been keeping me awake night after night.
Executive #2: Why don't you try my SCRUPLES? It's the one indiscretion remedy I can always rely on to prevent me from doing things I might later regret. In fact, it's got the exact same active ingredient found in the prescription brand PROHIBITOL.

(One week later)

Executive #2: I have to hand it to you, Phil. The boss seemed really impressed with your presentation at today's meeting.

Executive #1: Well, I've got you to thank. Since you got me taking SCRUPLES, I've never slept better in my life.

Announcer: Just two little SCRUPLES...and in no time at all, you'll be sleeping with a clear conscience again.

And, ultimately, this:

Announcer: How do you spell "belief"?

Televangelist: The only way, the way I do—Z-E-A-L-A-I-D-S.

Announcer: Plagued by doubt, skepticism and uncertainty? Unable to find the one true path to spiritual salvation? Then it's time for you to put whatever remaining faith you have in ZEALAIDS.

Ecstatic parishioner: I found ZEALAIDS; now I'm a believer. (Puts $10,000 check in collection plate.)

Announcer: Once you've swallowed a couple of ZEALAIDS, you'll be able to swallow just about anything.

DOING JUSTICE TO THE PRESIDENCY

(Originally published in The Berkshire Eagle, March 1988)

It's almost that time again—that time when millions of Americans who are almost totally preoccupied with such mundane matters as trying to make a living, trying to make ends meet, trying to make their kids behave, trying to make themselves appear younger, trendier or sexier, or simply trying to make it through the day will also be asked to make a momentous decision.

Without being required to know anything in particular, or even in general, about the backgrounds, beliefs or qualifications of the individuals involved, they'll once again be charged with the elective task of electing a president.

This "popular mandate" approach to choosing a chief executive/commander-in-chief might have sounded like an enlightened enough idea when it was tried back in the 19th Century. But is it really appropriate to an age when the choice can have such profound repercussions and when the office itself is the only one in the nation that remains vested with the authority to order civilization blown out of the water?

I think not. It seems to me that the time for such a casual, slipshod evaluation of supreme leadership ability is long past, and that doing justice to the highest office in the land calls for the same standards of painstaking, objective scrutiny that we require in seeking justice under the law.

In short, I think it would be in society's best interest if we were to compel our presidential candidates to abandon the antiquated campaign trail in favor of a campaign *trial* instead. That is, rather than having them make appearances for the purpose of courting the electorate, they ought to be compelled to appear in court for a thorough assessment of their competency and the various charges brought against them by their rivals for the job.

REPEAT OFFENDERS

By insisting that all aspirants take the stand instead of the stump and take an oath to tell the whole truth so help them God prior to taking any oath of office, we could be more reasonably assured that whoever was selected out of the lineup would be getting what they deserved. We could also feel more secure in the knowledge that all pertinent evidence and testimony to that effect was being meticulously examined by a jury of our peers—one sequestered from both everyday distractions and such prejudicial influences as paid political ads, editorial comments, tabloid exposes and polls reflecting whose bandwagon was in the lead at any given time.

Jury selection, of course, would be of critical importance to the validity of such a tribunal. To make sure all interest groups were fairly represented, jurors would have to be carefully chosen so as to reflect the makeup of the population as closely as possible in terms of things like gender, ethnicity, party affiliation, geography and economic status. A typical presidential jury might thus include, for example, a Jewish grandmother from Miami Beach, a WASP banking executive from New England, a Hispanic autoworker, a wealthy Republican rancher from Wyoming and a black female college professor.

Once assembled in this fashion, the panel could initially be split along party lines for a preliminary (or primary) hearing phase of the proceedings. During this stage, jurors would be given several months in which to exhaustively review every last excruciating detail of the case for and against each declared candidate, ranging from "prior convictions" to questions of character raised by things like extramarital affairs to evidence of precisely what an individual knew about any given situation and when he or she first knew it.

The entire jury could then be brought together for an extensive cross-examination of the two contenders found most competent to stand trial, each of whom would be given perhaps two hours tops to deliver their closing arguments. A final decision could then be rendered by simple majority vote.

One having heard the verdict, the presiding judge (perhaps a U.S. Supreme Court justice not appointed by an incumbent seeking re-election), following mandatory sentencing rules, would have no choice but to order the person charged with responsibility for leading the nation to report on the following January 20th to the maximum-security facility located at 1600 Pennsylvania Ave. in Washington, D.C., to begin serving a term of office not to exceed four years.

The advantages of such a system are obvious. Not only would it save the taxpayers untold millions of dollars currently wasted on campaign costs and related expenses, but it would keep any special interests from influencing the outcome of the race and give each hopeful a chance to be judged strictly on individual merit, rather than such superficial factors as name recognition, financial clout and organizational strength.

But best of all, it would relegate the selection of the nation's chief executive and top military commander to a group of people who could give the job the full attention it deserves—and allow the rest of us to devote ours to far less important things.

GUNS AND BUTTER

(Originally published in The Berkshire Eagle, September 1987)

When Irwin Schiff, a portly Big Apple businessman who reportedly "loved to eat" was gunned down recently while polishing off a meal at the Upper East Side restaurant where he reportedly loved to eat most, two resulting developments made the wire services.

One was the launching of an investigation into what connections the high-living, high-rolling and big-tipping Schiff may have had with the Mafia and, according to some sources, the FBI as well.

The other was the effect that the gangland-style killing had on the patronage of the restaurant itself, a small Italian eatery named Bravo Sergio.

I don't mean the immediate effect, which was to empty the establishment of all twenty or so of Schiff's fellow diners, including his blonde companion whom police were unable to locate for three days. I'm rather referring to the subsequent impact of the slaying on Bravo Sergio's business.

Regarded as an intimate little neighborhood restaurant prior to Schiff's demise, it has since achieved the status of a culinary landmark, attracting scores of new customers whose appetites (whether for food, violence, or both) seem to have been significantly whetted by the grisly incident. In fact, a number of individuals were said to have expressed disappointment when they were unable to find the departed diner's preferences on the menu displayed in the window.

While Bravo Sergio may not be the first New York City bistro to have had a patron get out of paying his tab in so decisive a manner, the widely publicized aftermath of this particular incident is one that is especially unlikely to escape the notice of restaurateurs seeking new insights into the kinds of things that turn on the dinner crowd.

REPEAT OFFENDERS

It might even prove to be the start of a whole new trend.

Envisioning potentially big bucks in the prospect of bullet-riddled customers slumped over their linguini and clam sauce, it seems only natural that some enterprising eatery operators will actively begin cultivating the kinds of clientele most apt to end up in this fashion. Meals and drinks on the house, for instance, could be offered to anyone able to produce a newspaper or magazine article identifying him as having links to organized crime or being the subject of a probe of mob-related activity.

Soon, encouraged by promoters for the restaurant industry (and perhaps even spurred along by a timely anonymous phone call now and then), underworld figures will be increasingly inclined to settle their scores during lunch or dinner hours at various culinary establishments—which will, in turn, begin proudly displaying photographs and other memorabilia of the victims and their untimely ends on their walls.

In time, a competition of sorts will commence heating up, as next to the little stars that various publications use to rate restaurants, little guns will be added to denote the current total of mob killings carried out on the premises.

Before long, patrons will be greeted by signs inviting them to 'dine at our death table" and menus will be featuring such specialties as "veal vendetta—an out-of-this-world experience."

Eventually, some establishments may even see fit to exploit their new-found notoriety by discarding traditional or long-familiar names in favor of such trendier themes as "Scene of the Crime," "The Rubout Room" and "Massacre II."

By then, of course, Madison Avenue will have gotten involved, as posh eateries begin to promote themselves in fashionable periodicals with a whole new assortment of advertising slogans, such as:

"Where getting a reservation can really be murder."

Or, "Some of the most influential hoods in town are dying to sample our cuisine."

Or, "We prepare every meal as if it were going to be your last."

SMOKING OUT NEW BUSINESS

*(Originally published in The Berkshire Eagle and
The SandPaper, March 1990)*

With all the badmouthing of cigarette manufacturers we've been hearing of late, it's easy to lose sight of the fact that tobacco was actually the oat bran of an earlier era.

Anyone who was around in the 1930s may recall some of the health benefits attributed to smoking in those days. If you're still around to recall them, in fact, one reason may be that you simply weren't as health conscious back then as cigarette manufacturers would have liked.

In 1936, for instance, the following remarks were attributed to "food editor" Dorothy Malone:

"My own personal experience is that smoking Camels with my meals and afterwards builds up a sense of digestive well-being."

That quote appeared within the context of a full page ad in the first issue of *Life* magazine—one detailing the traditional joys of an all-American Thanksgiving dinner, complete with cigarettes that the text urged be smoked both before and after each course "for digestion's sake."

No such claims, of course, can be found in today's pitches for tobacco. A close examination of Camels' current ad campaign, in fact, appears to actually contain a subliminal message (in addition to the mandatory one) about the potentially harmful effects of smoking. I'm referring to the "Joe Camel" character, which never struck me as representing an actual camel, but something more on the order of a 'camel-man'—an illustration of the type of fetal damage that might result from a woman continuing to smoke during pregnancy.

But because Joe is a cartoon character, the campaign that features him has been interpreted by some as pandering to the kiddie market—

which is understandable, since its sponsor, R.J. Reynolds Tobacco Co., was previously accused of attempting to target-market African Americans with a brand called Uptown and young women with another dubbed Dakota.

By utilizing a more sensitive and sensible approach, however, the tobacco industry could easily steer clear of such controversy without having to give up target marketing at all. It need only concentrate its efforts on those markets most ideally suited to its products—and still ripe for further cultivation.

Take habitual gamblers, for example. Not only do the risky propositions that are so much a part of their daily lives often tend to include smoking (as a visit to a casino or racetrack will readily confirm), but they also comprise a cross-section of virtually all socioeconomic and ethnic groups, excluding only those of tender age. Thus unhampered by the appearance of attempting to entice youths and minorities, winning ad campaigns could be developed for such speculative new brands as Touts ("the odds-on favorite of those in the know"), Longshots ("when you refuse to follow the crowd"), and Crapshoot ("for people who believe in taking their chances").

Another category of individuals with a reputation for high-risk ventures is that commonly referred to as "organized crime." Surely, no one would be likely to call it foul play if some enterprising tobacco operation were to target its members with such bold new products as Magnum ("a real hit with families like yours") or False ("for an unbelievably refreshing break in the testimony"). There's simply no telling how potentially lucrative such an aggressive attempt to acquire new turf might prove.

Not to be overlooked, of course, is that elite group for whom tobacco use is a time-honored tradition. Indeed, if whether or not to smoke be a matter of individual choice, it is our politicians above all others who would appear most capable of exercising their right to decide whether such special-interest brands as Caucus ("the leading contributor to a majority of smoke-filled rooms") or Referendum ("strongest PAC, longest recess") are worth allocating money and taxing their health for.

And while we're on the subject of tradition, could there be any more universally recognized than the sacred right of the condemned man to one last cigarette? Perhaps nowhere in today's world is the appeal of nicotine addiction less cruel and more usual than on death row. What could possibly be the harm of recognizing the spark of humanity that continues to burn within its inmates, even as they fight to keep the switch from being pulled, by making available to them such alternatives as Swan Song ("for when life becomes a drag"), Last Roundup ("doing it your way") and Lights Out ("dead with pleasure").

We've come a long way since the days when smoking was seen as a healthy practice. But that doesn't mean for a moment that it can't continue to be viewed as a source of healthy profits.

EXPORTING RUBBISH

(Originally published in The Berkshire Eagle, April 1987)

Considering the fact that, implied promises notwithstanding, we long ago ran short of accommodations for their tired, poor and huddled masses yearning to breathe free, it should come as no great surprise to us when some of our less fortunate neighbors fail to roll out any red carpets for the wretched refuse of our own teeming shore.

Nevertheless, when the likes of Mexico, Belize and the Bahamas have the unmitigated gall to actually send packing some 3,100 tons of garbage thrown away in the U.S.A. on our very first attempt to export the stuff, that could well prove to be the start of an extremely messy situation for us just down the road.

It's one thing for Florida, North Carolina and various Gulf Coast states to raise a mild stink over the prospect of becoming dumping grounds for locales like Islip, New York. But when struggling nations begin to get the idea that they can simply turn up their noses at the waste products of our affluent society, perhaps it's time we began considering the various courses of action open to us in getting such "refuse-niks" to wake up and smell the coffee grounds.

And, make no mistake about it, there are some very effective means at our disposal for saddling them with the entire mess (so what are a few more flies to such places?) before we find ourselves faced with the unpleasant alternative of having to designate the Grand Canyon as a national public landfill.

We could, for instance, always resort to our basic prerogative of threatening them with a cutoff of American aid money—in other words, no more cash unless you accept our trash.

Or, perhaps better yet from a diplomatic perspective, the garbage itself could be dispensed as a form of additional aid—particularly to countries where the debris of a comparatively opulent culture might substantially improve the lot of many inhabitants whose subsistence is currently drawn from picking through home-grown rubbish heaps.

Then again, we might try the "munitions dump" approach, in which arms shipments sold to foreign countries could be buried beneath sizable quantities of refuse, which the recipients would have no choice but to unload upon delivery (and which, under certain combat conditions, might even have a practical military application in the erection of defensive fortifications).

Ultimately, we might even find it to our advantage to 'trash' our adversaries abroad instead of bombing them. Dumping a few thousand tons of U.S. garbage on various strategic targets, including the headquarters of leaders who have rubbed us the wrong way, could send them a very potent message that they'd better get busy cleaning up their act—without all the negative repercussions and criticism that lethal and destructive air raids tend to create.

If we'd simply stay cool and use our heads before deciding to send any more garbage scows off willy-nilly into international waters, we'd find there are all kinds of clever ways we could palm off our discarded stuff on underprivileged societies—and come out smelling like a rose.

TRIALS AND ERRORS

A LESSON IN CIVILITY

(Originally published in The Berkshire Eagle, October 1991)

A lot of parents these days may think that just because they've reached a certain age, that somehow gives them a perfect right to sass their kids.

Adults who up until now have gotten away with such impudence, however, may be in for a rude awakening. At long last, our society appears at the point of being fed up with the blatant disrespect frequently exhibited toward children by their elders.

In fact, those who engage in this sort of insolent behavior may now find themselves having to face some serious consequences—like a couple of days' confinement to a locked room in the local house of detention, for instance.

That's precisely the type of punishment that was meted out recently by a Nashville, Tennessee, magistrate to country singer Lynn Anderson for her alleged audacity in cussing out her 12-year-old son and 10-year-old daughter during a court-appointed visit.

"This kind of conduct on her part has got to cease," warned Circuit Judge Muriel Robinson Rice, who, while staying the sentence pending an appeal, quite aptly demonstrated how a display of contempt for one's offspring might actually be interpreted as contempt of court.

Many will no doubt applaud such mature judicial reasoning as being long overdue. It's bad enough after all, that today's youngsters have to be exposed to so much vile language in movies and on television, from their friends, and in the lyrics of rap and heavy metal (or whatever name might be attached to the latest form of popular discord). They certainly shouldn't have to put up with it from, of all people, their very own parents.

It wasn't always so, of course. One need look no further back down the road than the 1950s to remember when grownups customarily

REPEAT OFFENDERS

employed kinder, gentler tones when addressing or admonishing those of tender age. Can you even conceive of anything remotely resembling an obscenity tumbling from the lips of a Ward Cleaver or an Ozzie and Harriet Nelson, even when faced with the most vexing of juvenile transgressions?

Within a decade, however, all that began to change, and it must be admitted that the kids themselves weren't entirely blameless. It was they, after all, who during the turbulent '60s often set a bad example for their parents—parents all too eager to mimic any form of behavior that might make them appear more youthful.

Not only did many youngsters allow themselves to become poor role models in their manner of self-expression, but they also managed to arouse feelings of resentment in adults by flaunting their ability to indulge in practices that were strictly off limits to most overage people, like smoking pot and protesting against the business establishment.

The result, not surprisingly, was that a substantial number of supposedly "mature" individuals began voicing open defiance of their children, which often took the form of expletives not suitable for a family newspaper. And the kids, in turn, reached adulthood believing that such utterances constituted a perfectly acceptable standard of parental behavior.

That's why the edict handed down by the Nashville jurist represents such a significant victory for those wishing to restore some measure of decorum to American family life. It's high time that some of today's mommies and daddies were taught this kind of lesson in court-ordered civility, with criminal penalties imposed on those who fail to keep a civil tongue and "repeat offenders" subject to even harsher sentences for their insistence on indulging in harsh words.

You can be sure that in the future, they'll be a lot more inclined to watch their mouths—and to exercise the self-discipline of just saying "no" when they might feel like saying a hell of a lot of other things.

WARDING OFF THE UNDERWORLD

(Originally published in The Berkshire Eagle, June 1989)

As if the nation's crime fighters didn't have enough to occupy their attention these days, a case now awaiting trial in Tupelo, Miss., could signify the re-emergence of a particularly diabolical brand of criminality, that was generally believed to have been successfully eradicated from our society a good many years ago.

It seems that the authorities down there have charged one John Henry Adams, along with his half-brother Leroy Ivy, of conspiracy to murder Circuit Judge Thomas Gardener III, who had earlier sentenced Adams to a 25-to-40-year term in the state penitentiary for armed robbery.

What makes this case particularly alarming, however, is the alleged nature of the conspiracy at issue. Specifically, the two defendants are accused of plotting to do away with the judge by having a hex put on him.

Prosecutors claim that the pair planned to send a faded photograph of Gardener that Ivy had purchased for $100, together with what was supposed to be a lock of the magistrate's hair, to a Jamaican voodoo priest, who was to have used the items to place a death curse on the jurist.

Despite their contention that the photo was merely intended for display on a punching bag Adams used in prison, the defendants were each held in lieu of $50,000 bond while awaiting trial before another magistrate. If convicted, they could each be sentenced to 20 years and fined up to $500,000 apiece.

Harsh as such penalties may appear to some, they're actually pretty lenient when compared with the way Massachusetts authorities once dealt with offenses in this very category that were far less serious in nature.

REPEAT OFFENDERS

Under their jurisdiction, simply being accused of an act as relatively trivial as putting a hex on your neighbor's cow would more than likely be sufficient to land you an appointment with the gallows (which was still a somewhat more humane form of punishment than the heat felt by those found guilty of similar transgressions in the Old World).

In retrospect, we are now able to more fully appreciate the long-term effectiveness of this no-nonsense approach to keeping society off limits to such pernicious underworld influences. Such stern measures, after all, appear to have succeeded in keeping a lid on the black arts in this country for an entire three centuries!

Lest we be lulled into complacency, however, the entire episode now unfolding in Mississippi should serve as an unmistakable warning of the perils still lurking just beneath the surface—demonic dangers that pose far more of a threat to our world than they did to folks living back in the 1690s.

For whereas in those simpler times there were limits to the amount of damage a curse could bring about. The potential results of such powers falling into the hands of today's sophisticated terrorists could be unspeakably disastrous. Never mind a judge, no chief of state, city or nuclear power plant would be safe from those having the wrong motives and the right supernatural connections.

Adding to our vulnerability on this score is the fact that, unlike the malefactors of early Massachusetts who pretty much did their own trafficking with the forces of evil, anyone desiring to put a quick curse on someone or something today has potential access to a growing culture of "hexperts" who, having received their training in voodoo in clandestine Caribbean enclaves, can readily make their services available for a fee.

That's why, if we're going to nip this satanic situation in the bud, we'll need to come down hard and fast on both the casual users of curses and those who actually conjure them up. To this end, concerted efforts will be required on the part of local, state and federal law-enforcement officials involving everything from forming special voodoo vice squads and creating a new government agency for the Investigation of Spells and Incantations to bringing back the death penalty for first-degree sorcery. No mere conventional witch-hunt, in other words, but rather something closer to a full-scale War on Witchcraft.

It may sound like a formidable task. But don't forget that there is a powerful weapon available to us—one that Western societies have been using as a deterrent to this sort of deviltry ever since the Dark Ages. I'm referring, of course, to the convention of establishing guilt by virtue of accusation alone.

While such a suggestion will no doubt raise the hackles of lily-livered liberal and ACLU types, there's simply too much at stake to allow them to undermine our ability to ward off this re-emerging underworld menace. Besides, where in the Constitution is it written that giving the devil his due should include giving those who consort with him the benefit of due process?

When you come right down to it, the policy of zero tolerance is one that hasn't been surpassed in 300 years.

SENSELESS VIOLENCE AND SENSIBLE VALUES

(Originally published in the Orlando Sentinel, November 1997)

Just when it appears that the American jury system ought to be relegated to the ash heap of jurisprudence—something that seems to occur with ever-increasing regularity these days—a decision is handed down that restores our confidence in the ability of a dozen ordinary citizens to interpret the laws of the land intelligently.

Such was the case in the heartland town of Bloomfield, Iowa, in which a jury recently spared two 18-year-olds the stigma of being branded serious criminals for the mere taking of baseball bats to some captive stray cats.

The most impressive thing about this particular panel, however, was the sound, practical process it used in determining that such feline-bashing wasn't felonious foul play on the part of those fellows but mere misdemeanor material—an approach that could prove to have far more profound applications.

What these jurors did was to sit down and calculate the actual damages that resulted when the overly exuberant youths broke into an animal shelter and used about two dozen cats for batting practice, 16 of whom failed to survive the encounter.

Refusing to be in any way influenced by the emotional excesses that took place in the town of Fairfield, where the incident occurred (and which caused the trial to be moved), the jury was able to determine that the actual amount of damage done by the lads was less than $500. That amount was based on a value of no more than $31.25 per cat (a generous figure, given the fact that there is no market for adult stray cats, as the defendants' lawyer was quick to point out).

"I understand it was a stupid, childish mistake," was how one 19-year-old juror put it. But, he added, "I don't think the 16 lives of the cats were worth $500, personally."

REPEAT OFFENDERS

And there's the point. All too often, prosecutors seeking convictions of those charged with violent acts attempt to appeal to jurors' emotions rather than their common sense. In doing so, they focus on the gory details while withholding crucial, bottom-line evidence that could provide the basis for a rational and dispassionate verdict, not to mention a punishment that fiscally fits the crime.

By applying the type of simple, clear-headed logic used by the Iowa cat-bashing jury to cases involving human victims, however, our entire justice system could be streamlined and purged of the erratic, capricious and unpredictable rulings that have given it such a bad reputation.

All we need do is what any good insurance company does when calculating the amount of tangible loss involved in a case of death or injury caused by the negligence of one of its clients. That is, determine just how specific a debt to society a violent criminal may have incurred in terms of actual dollars and cents.

Adopting such a formula would soon make it apparent that the great majority of murders aren't in fact all that serious, because most victims come from lower-income groups with little or no earning potential and, hence, negligible cash value (many, in fact, actually constituting a burden to society by virtue of being on welfare or Social Security).

Carrying it one step further, we could quantify these findings in terms of a point system that would provide judges with a mandatory standard for meting out sentences.

Let's say, for instance, that every $1,000 lost in terms of the market value of victims' lives translated into a month's incarceration. Then the cost of killing some poor or unemployable individual whose existence was appraised at no more than $12,000 would be only a year's confinement, whereas doing in a big, corporate executive earning, say, $500,000 a year plus stock options automatically would get you life with no chance for parole. Nor would there by any further need to worry about such mitigating or aggravating factors as motive, which could be neatly dispensed with in a judicial adaptation of the "flat-tax" concept.

Not only would such a system bring about a more consistent standard of justice and ease the burden on our criminal courts, but it would act as a deterrent to violent crime in more-affluent neighborhoods by making its perpetrators feel less at risk confining their anti-social activities to inner cities, where they belong. Ultimately, it could help our suburbs once again to become the safe and secure havens they were intended to be.

Such are the potential benefits to society revealed by those astute Iowa jurors, who have shown us how justice can be achieved through the application of simple, sensible values to senseless acts of violence—and how it's still apparently possible to find a dozen people in one locale whose friends and families don't include a single feline.

CRACKING DOWN ON PETTY PHILANTHROPY

(Originally published in The SandPaper, February 1997)

Now that conventional crime rates are supposedly on the decline, it's gratifying to learn that our police and courts are finally able to turn their attention to a particularly deplorable form of antisocial activity that up to now has been largely overlooked.

At long last, America's criminal justice system appears to have begun cracking down on those dangerously depraved petty philanthropists who go around committing random acts of kindness—the kind that, if allowed to go unchecked, have the potential to make contemporary urban existence even less viable than it already is.

In a case recently heard in a Cincinnati courtroom, just such an offender—not untypically a woman—was convicted of a misdemeanor after being caught in the act of putting change into two expired parking meters, apparently to spare perfect strangers the expense of a parking ticket.

The defendant, one Sylvia Stayton, a 63-year-old grandmother of 10, was characterized by her lawyer as someone simply "doing a good deed"—and, as might be expected, managed to evoke the bleeding-heart sympathies of other misguided do-gooders, some of whom even raised money for her legal expenses.

But let's examine for a moment what would happen if Stayton were allowed to get away with behavior of this sort, inspiring similarly twisted individuals to give vent to such two-bit charitable impulses anytime they felt like it.

Imagine if you will, the impact on a city suddenly deprived of one of its most dependable sources of revenue—overtime parking fines. Adding to the overall fiscal crisis would be the numerous individual ones created by the necessity of having to lay off possibly dozens of meter attendants, many with families to support.

Beyond such obvious repercussions, however, would be the other long-term hidden costs—the disappearance, for instance, of one of society's chief means of maintaining a sense of order, discipline and punctuality.

The fact is that without forceful reminders such as those imposed by parking-meter deadlines and sure-fire penalties for allowing them to lapse, citizens themselves would lapse into laggardness and tend to lose their awareness of time. The inevitable result: large numbers of personal and professional schedules gone awry, heightening existing levels of economic and family instability.

The physical health and fitness of the population would suffer as well from the loss of forced regular exercise that would occur once men and women no longer felt compelled to dash back to their cars to deposit extra coins, secure in the knowledge that some pathologically considerate soul would do it for them.

But worse yet would be the psychological impact that such a presumption would undoubtedly have on countless individuals, leading them into destructive patterns of dependency on the kindness of strangers. At a time when our national emphasis is on getting people off welfare by making them more self-reliant, a trend of this sort could hardly come as a more unwelcome development.

Indeed, were this case an isolated one, merely limited to one woman's warped motivations, perhaps we could afford to take a more lenient view of her misdeeds. As it turns out, however, the problem appears to run far deeper, reflected in the creation of "Sylvia Stayton…guilty of kindness" T-shirts by a church group, which, by its own admission, has been anonymously feeding parking meters for years.

Given the appalling potentials for harm inherent in such unsolicited beneficence, one can only hope that the court sees fit to impose the maximum penalty for her crime—a $750 fine and three months confinement in jail—in order to send the strongest possible "zero-tolerance" message to all such aberrant altruists. One might also hope that her 10 grandchildren will be dissuaded from following their grandmother down that all-too-familiar good-intention-paved path by realizing that while virtue may be its own reward, it can also be a highly punishable offense.

Perhaps most important, though, is to get people like Stayton off the street—or sidewalk—and behind bars where they not only belong, but can do the most good. Because is there's anything this country desperately needs right now, it's a kinder, gentler inmate population for its rapidly expanding penal institutions.

GUARDING YOUR FUTURE

(Originally published in The SandPaper, April 1997)

These days it seems you simply can't trust anybody.

Not the surgeon who may be removing your gall bladder without actually having a license to operate. Not the insurance company that tries to persuade you to unknowingly cheat yourself by changing your coverage in mid-life. And certainly not the "contractor" who just happened to be driving by and noticed your driveway desperately needed sealing and is ready and willing to do the job for you on the spot at a price so low it's laughable.

All that might be bad enough. But the growing erosion of confidence in professional integrity has now reached the point of becoming attached to one of our most ancient and honorable vocations. Lamentably, the traditional Gypsy fortuneteller is now among those to be swept up in the general climate of distrust and suspicion.

The problem is that some of these soothsayers have apparently opted to abuse their psychic powers by fleecing patrons out of their fortunes rather than simply reading them.

A recent example was a gentleman of Gypsy descent who was sentenced to 34 months by a federal magistrate for what a newspaper headline termed "fortune-telling fraud." The defendant, in fact, admitted to bilking a young heiress out of a $100,000 inheritance when she paid a visit to Madame Flora's, a prognosticating parlor actually run by his father-in-law.

The victim in this case had reportedly gone to the establishment for counseling about her legacy, only to be told that it was causing her to radiate negative energy resulting from an unhappy former life too focused on material possessions, and that relinquishing the money to Madame Flora would cause the bad vibes to disappear along with it.

Other reports have depicted mendacious mediums as warning

REPEAT OFFENDERS

clients that the only way to remove a curse was to hand over their savings—said curse being duly dispensed with, of course, as soon as the customer complied.

Now, you might think that one has to first seek out a seer in order to fall victim to such schemes. But I foresee a situation arising in which you can be hoodwinked right in your own home, without ever having solicited psychic assistance.

For just as sure as the authorities are to tighten their surveillance of palm readers, crystal gazers and the like, the less than scrupulous among them will take to the open road. And, as I ponder this, I predict that sooner or later, you'll be receiving a visit from one of these charismatic characters. And when you do, the person you must learn to trust least is yourself.

For while you might consider yourself far too streetwise to fall for a driveway-sealing scam, you actually may be a lot more gullible than you think when it comes to dealing with a dishonest diviner, whether it be a genuine Gypsy or somebody posing as one.

In fact, you may be surprised at how quickly you'll find yourself suspending all rational judgment, trotting down to the bank, withdrawing large sums from your savings account and forking them over to some corrupt clairvoyant.

The bottom line is that you're in real danger of being taken to the cleaners by a seasoned bunko artist—that is, unless you allow me to come to your aid.

Now ordinarily, I'm quite content to remain an observer of the human condition and to refrain from becoming personally involved in other people's problems. But I also believe there are times when, seeing an imminent crisis looming, one has a moral obligation to step in and render assistance.

I'd therefore like to make you a generous offer of help in guarding your future. All you do to avail yourself of it is to temporarily transfer your funds into my protective custody (a simple cashier's check should suffice) so they won't be accessible to you when some fortune-telling fraud perpetrator succeeds in breaking down your resistance.

You can rest assure that I won't fall for any of the clever little ploys they might attempt, such as convincing you to use some pretext to talk me into giving you back the money ("I need it to pay the mortgage" being a typical such ruse). In fact, I promise not to return it until I've definitely divined that the danger has passed.

And, yes, there will come a time in the not-too-distant future when your trust will be restored—not only in fortunetellers, but also in surgeons, insurance-company representatives, home-repair contractors and the numerous other professionals whose honesty we've come to question. You can take it from me.

What you want to avoid is having them take it from you in the meantime.

ANECDOTAL ANOMALIES

BACK ON THE FRONT BURNERS OF HISTORY

(Originally published in The Record of Bergen County, N.J., and The Philadelphia Inquirer, June 2005)

As someone who wasn't born yesterday, I sometimes suspect that I'm the target of a vast, youth-culture conspiracy bent on relegating me to obsolescence.

The feeling was perhaps most aptly described by my sister (who's a good deal younger than I), as one of having awakened from a long sleep to find there's a whole new crop of celebrities and having absolutely no idea who they are.

But lately I find I've been able to deep-six the unsettling sensation of being adrift in an alien sea. In fact, I'm suddenly feeling very much back in vogue, as "in with the in crowd" as ever—all thanks to a couple of guys who, at least for a few moments, caught the media's attention.

While I once couldn't have imagined myself expressing gratitude to a G-man—especially an ally of J. Edgar Hoover's—my broad-brimmed hat is off (or would be, if I still owned one) to Mark Felt. By having tottered forward to reveal himself as the mysterious Deep Throat of the Watergate saga, the aging ex-agent and one-time number two man at the FBI has achieved spectacular success in turning our attention back to those thrilling days of yesteryear when the biggest of all enchiladas could be brought down by a couple of well-aimed journalistic slingshots.

Thanks to his having waited so long to reveal himself, those of us who lived through that period no longer need feel like a bunch of outmoded outsiders. Virtually overnight, what we know and when we knew it have been infused with immediacy—and all in regard to a matter of which many members of the youth culture seem to know little or nothing, such events having been, in their own parlance, before their time.

True, Bob Woodward, who gave Deep Throat notoriety as the

REPEAT OFFENDERS

Father of All Anonymous Sources, may continue to be a best-seller-list presence. But mention "Woodward and Bernstein" to those younger than 30, and you're apt to evoke as uncomprehending an expression as you would by talking to them about Simon and Garfunkel.

For me in particular, however, there's more to it than the sense of having the history-making events of one's life put back on the front burners by those who determine what's cooking on a daily basis. While my newspaper career never directly involved any Watergate-related reporting, I later had the opportunity to meet and interview Frank Sturgis, one of the burglars who set the whole series of events in motion (not that I should be letting you in on who he was if you didn't already know).

The focus of the interview, however, was on another subject—what Sturgis claimed was Castro's involvement in the JFK assassination, a crime in which many believe Sturgis was one of the participants. (He did tell me to investigate should he ever be run over by a truck, but since he reportedly ended up dying of natural causes and there appeared to be no smoking gun, I decided it might be best not to go looking for one.)

But if the hoopla over the revelation of Deep Throat's identity weren't enough to restore my faltering sense of connection with the here and now, along came yet another fortuitous bolt from the blue in the person of disputed U.N. ambassador nominee John Bolton. Inspired by the characterization of Bolton as the quintessential boss from hell, the subject of dealing with raging supervisors has suddenly become the rage—and one to which I can also readily relate.

That's because it was only a few years ago, while serving in a managerial position, that I found myself working under a "bully boss" myself—and I've been positively delighted to discover how perfectly this individual fit the profile of someone who kisses up to superiors while engaging in consistently abusive behavior toward underlings.

For the first time, in fact, I realize that what I experienced in that job (as did predecessors with whom I subsequently compared notes) was part of a pattern that seems to pervade the American workplace, and against which employees in this country seem to have little legal recourse.

But I'm afraid that, like Deep Throat, the identity of the individual involved (as well as the company) will have to remain undisclosed for the indeterminate future, lest I should happen to encounter her in a hotel corridor somewhere and again find myself the target of a torrent of expletives of the sort that would ordinarily be deleted from a family newspaper.

I can, however, thank Mark Felt and John Bolton for making me feel I'm no longer living on the fringe of an alien culture. For a few brief, shining weeks, at least, I can honestly say I know what the in crowd knows.

THE TWO-CENT REFUND THAT
REDEEMED MY SENSE OF SELF-WORTH

(Originally published in The Record of Bergen County, N.J., October 2005)

In the world of finance, I play a role that is admittedly penny-ante. And I'm not engaging in mere hyperbole when I say that, being the kind of guy who doesn't hesitate to pick up a penny whenever I spot one on the theory that a cent a day accumulated in this way can amount to $3.65 a year in extra earnings (reasoning with which I know Ben Franklin would nod heartily in agreement).

Still, I've always been acutely cognizant of having been distinctly out of the monetary mainstream, where speculating in spectacular sums is the stock in trade of wheeler-dealers and corporate bottom lines routinely run into the billions of dollars.

Or at least I thought I was—that is, until coming into possession of a check from that telecommunications colossus Verizon, payable through Fleet Bank.

Labeled "refund account," it was (or is, being still in my possession) made out in the amount of "zero and 02/100 dollars."

For those of you who may have had trouble with fractions in grade school, that's a whole two cents—a sum not worth nearly as much as it once was, due to a combination of inflation and the fact that pre-1982 pennies were made mostly of copper, whereas those minted since consist of a much cheaper zinc alloy.

Overcome by curiosity as to the nature of the indebtedness that had resulted in this unexpected windfall, I endeavored to make some inquiries as to what specifically had prompted it. Initially, with a little help from the Internet, I did succeed in coming up with a number for the Verizon office in Richmond, Virginia, that was listed as the return address on the check, only to have my attempts to contact it during the next couple of days greeted by a recurrent busy signal.

REPEAT OFFENDERS

Finally, I took it upon myself to contact the company's headquarters using a number I had managed to find in a previous attempt to register a complaint, whereupon I proceeded to explain to a representative that I was trying to determine exactly what the two-cent refund was for.

While not authorized to offer an official explanation, she did informally inform me that Verizon is obliged to make many such refunds "for whatever reasons." So many refunds, in fact, that the department involved "specifically told us that they can't respond to the overwhelming number of people calling" about them.

She was willing to say the amount of the refund may have seemed a tad unusual, but she attributed that small anomaly to a totally computerized operation that routinely "spit out" such checks without imposing any value judgments on them. Had the company been a smaller one she confided, a check for so trivial a sum would probably not have been generated.

If that's the case, it could open up a whole range of new image-building and promotional possibilities for the company. For example, "At Verizon, we can account for every last penny." Or perhaps "We're the one telecommunications company that can always be depended on to give you your two cents' worth." Or what about "Verizon: The bigger we get, the smaller the details we're able to manage"?

As for that check in the amount of zero and 0.02 dollars—well, there's just no way we can bring ourselves to cash it, despite being sorely tempted to take that refund straight down to the penny slots now being advertised by some Atlantic City casinos. (Hey, I did once win $80 on two nickels I just happened to have in my pocket.) It's just too good a conversation piece when people drop by.

And though it may be only a two-cent refund, it's one that has yielded a distinctly improved sense of my self-worth. Because even though finding a penny a day may not keep penury away, I can now consider myself every bit as penny-wise as a corporation worth billions of dollars every time I stoop to pick one up.

INADVERTENT INTERNET IDENTITY THEFT, PART I

(Originally published in The Philadelphia Inquirer, December 2002)

Unlike some individuals—not least among them Pulitzer Prize-winning historian Joseph Ellis—I make no pretensions of ever having served in the armed forces.

Though it might enhance my image and standing in the community, I could never be accused of allowing myself to be mistaken for a veteran.

But a veterinarian—well, that's another story.

Let's just say I never deliberately set out to provide myself with bogus credentials in this field. It just sort of happened, in spite of my best efforts to always be on the up-and-up and avoid any hint of fabrication about my background and accomplishments.

Exactly how it happened, I'm still not sure, although I feel confident that someone versed in the finer points of computer technology (your average 12-year-old, perhaps) could offer me a reasonable explanation. But whatever the reason, the result is that an unspecified number of former classmates of mine from high school and college are now probably under the misapprehension that my career has been devoted to the noble practice of administering to and saving the lives of people's beloved pets (not to mention performing spaying and neutering procedures).

And that would seem like a reasonable enough assumption, based on my supposedly having been a member of the University of Pennsylvania School of Veterinary Medicine's 1980 graduating class.

When I first stumbled upon this surprise embellishment to the educational information I had provided to the Classmates Internet service (the Web's answer to a strange impulse that arises in middle age to communicate with people one could once barely tolerate), I was a bit dumbfounded, I must say.

REPEAT OFFENDERS

At first, the thought even crossed my mind that perhaps, in recognition of my years of selfless dedication to the care and feeding of (and cleaning up after) a progression of dogs and cats, the university had seen fit to confer on me an honorary degree, but somehow failed to inform me.

But that notion was immediately dispelled by the realization that this would have happened 22 years ago, when I was a lot less qualified for such a distinction than I am now.

I was thus left to conclude that the data had been 'doctored' through an electronic error. It became all the more apparent when a further check revealed that I apparently had been 'cyberconfused' (for want of a better word) with someone who had, in fact, earned a veterinary degree.

Admittedly, the idea that people I once knew may have been given a fallacious impression of what I do for a living is a tad unsettling to my sense of truth and accuracy. But what I find even more disturbing are the implications of such an occurrence in light of developments in the country's war on terrorism.

From what I've been reading, the authorities in charge of homeland security have been granted broad powers to collect information on people. A "Total Information Awareness" program, for instance, will allow the Defense Department to develop dossiers of data on millions of citizens, using a variety of public, private and commercial sources.

While civil libertarians voice alarm over the potential mass invasion of privacy, my concern is for what happens when such screw-ups are codified and compounded by government bureaucrats.

Might some individuals secretly be placed under surveillance as security risks by virtue of occupations or affiliations that have been mistakenly attributed to them due to computer glitches, human error, or a combination of the two? For example, could a sojourn at the Better-Living Institute be misreported as an extended visit to a Bin Laden training camp?

And, conversely, might those who represent real threats to the country be mistakenly passed off as model citizens via the unquestioning acceptance of, say, an inaccurate reference to them studying for a doctorate at Yale, while they were really busy studying terror tactics under the Taliban?

I'm afraid only time will tell. In the meantime, rest assured that I won't be administering any rabies shots—or attempting to perform any lifesaving surgery on your dog or cat.

INADVERTENT INTERNET IDENTITY THEFT, PART II

(Originally published in the Philadelphia Inquirer, March 2006)

Is Jason Smith out there?

I don't mean just any Jason Smith. The Jason Smith I'm looking for reportedly graduated a number of years ago from the University of Pennsylvania School of Veterinary Medicine.

I say "reportedly" because my source has proved to be less than reliable. But I'll get to that in a moment.

If this Jason Smith is aware of this attempt to reach him, he needs to get in touch with me ASAP. The reason is that I seem to have inadvertently assumed his identity—and vice versa.

I initially wrote about this muddle three years ago, upon discovering that the Classmates.com web site had mistakenly attributed to me a veterinary degree from the school in question (which I had no recollection of attending, let alone graduating from).

I noted how misinformation of this sort, disseminated over the Internet, could fall into the wrong hands—such as federal snoops compiling dossiers on people they suspect of being potential terrorists.

I subsequently discovered that my school records had somehow become electronically entangled with those of a veterinary school alumnus named Jason Smith, and I made attempts to notify the operators of the Classmates site to that effect.

But rather than acknowledging their mistake and correcting it, the Classmates crew (whom I'll get to in a moment) compounded it in odd ways.

For one thing, it changed my name to "Jason" in messages relating to my real alma mater in New London, Conn. Such missives, which I receive regularly, now typically contain subject headings such as, "Jason, read what's new in the Mitchell College message board."

REPEAT OFFENDERS

Upon further examination, I have discovered that my official Classmates "profile" is listed under "Jason Smith (Bonvie)."

While I can understand how a case of mistaken identity might migrate to other destinations along the misinformation superhighway, I'm at a loss to explain other e-mails I've received from Classmates.

I'm talking about the ones addressed to "Bill."

For the record, you should know (and I'm trusting you not to misuse this information) that just before my 14th birthday, my family moved from Connecticut to Florida, where I subsequently graduated from Winter Park High School.

Although I returned to Connecticut to attend college and even lived there for a time, I can't recall spending so much as a day in a high school there.

So how is it, I wonder, that Classmates now sends me communications (under my actual name) urging me to get in touch with people in my New London (Conn.) High School graduating class?

What might be next? I wonder. Can I expect to start receiving e-mails urging Adm. Jason Bonvie to get in touch with his fellow graduates of yet another New London institution, the U.S. Coast Guard Academy?

In any event, I would like to know more about these people who keep insisting, despite my efforts to inform them otherwise, that I'm somebody I'm not or spent my youth attending an institution in which I've never set foot.

Are they a bunch of practical jokers having a good laugh at my (and Jason Smith's) expense? Or are they clandestine agents trying to reinvent my life and/or identity for devious purposes, as was done to ad man Roger Thornhill in Alfred Hitchcock's *North by Northwest*?

Then there's the possibility, no matter how far-fetched it sounds, that they're not people at all.

Perhaps Classmates is nothing more than a mainframe computer, sitting alone in an electronic enclave somewhere, spitting out cockamamie correspondence to a database consisting of graduates of the nation's secondary schools and colleges.

If so, perhaps the key to eliciting a response to my complaints might be to inform the source that I am aware of its true identity. So the next time I get one of Classmates' muddled e-mails, I'll begin my reply, "Dear HAL..."

Author's note: Since the preceding two essays originally appeared, Facebook has become for many of us the preferred method of getting back in touch with one's old classmates. But that has by no means eliminated electronic errors that can result in maddening misrepresentations of one's personhood. Not long ago, for example, I received several "home page" messages to the effect that a friend (and former classmate), whom I know to be an ardent environmentalist, "liked" the public relations blurbs being disseminated on Facebook by BP. Perplexed, I finally queried her about it via e-mail, resulting in her posting a message to all her Facebook friends noting that she actually hated the petro-giant responsible for the huge Gulf of Mexico oil spill and never given its promotional messages any such endorsement.

SEGREGATION OF LAWYERS:
IT'S NO JOKE

*(Originally published in the Orlando Sentinel,
April 1999)*

Heard about the lawyer who sued a developer for canceling an agreement to sell him a home in a subdivision upon learning that he was a lawyer?

Turns out the developer didn't want to sell to any lawyers who might subsequently threaten to sue him.

Think that's another one of those lawyer jokes, do you? No, my friend, this story, which comes out of Bakersfield, California, is perfectly legit. In other words, it's not meant to be funny—and if you think it is anyway, that merely indicates your acquiescence in the anti-lawyer bias that is already creating such a deep division within our society.

Just how much of a rift is reflected by the developer in question, whose own lawyer (talk about being a traitor to one's trade!) responded to the suit with a letter stating that the firm's "experience is that home buyers who are also lawyers threaten litigation…at a dramatically higher rate than home buyers who are not lawyers."

What's next? A "non-lawyers only" country club, perhaps?

As someone who holds members of the legal profession in the highest esteem—some of my best friends, in fact, are lawyers—I feel compelled after reading this little news item to challenge some of the irrational assumptions that are now causing those people to become the latest victims of discrimination in America.

To begin with, the notion that attorneys stand ready to sue at the drop of a hat—or, in this case, the settling of a house (hoping ultimately to settle out of court)—is just plain ludicrous. In fact, if anyone is in a position to know the actual time and effort involved in filing a questionable or frivolous lawsuit, it's someone who does it for a living—the reason most lawyers want big retainers up front for anything that doesn't guarantee a sure-fire judgment from which they can extract their third of the proceeds.

Far more likely to haul someone into court is some mild-mannered, retired English teacher determined to redress some minor grievance or other with absolutely no understanding of just how valuable a lawyer's time actually is, or of how many years, motions and legal maneuvers winning a case might end up requiring.

Such misconceptions, however, simply give rise to other dubious reasons to bar members of the bar from neighborhoods of their own choosing—an example being the theory that property values tend to decline the minute one moves in.

Now, it may well be true that having an attorney take possession of the house next door could conceivably cause some homeowners to hastily put up "for sale" signs, based on fears of an impending invasion of process servers. But by the same token, the threatening aura created by having one or more lawyers in residence tends to discourage local authorities from allowing such value-impacting facilities as sewage plants, landfills and prisons to be developed on any nearby, less stringently zoned tracts.

Then, too, it's important to remember that today's super-high real-estate prices might never have evolved in the first place were it not for the generous spending habits of well-heeled lawyers, who, together with professional stock traders, deserve much of the credit for keeping housing costs hugely inflated in a kind of residential "trickle-down" process.

There's also the ignorant belief being bandied about in some quarters that lawyers as a group are far more likely than other professionals to engage in unlawful activities. Such maligning is the result of years of news media stereotyping, which has consistently portrayed members of the legal community as being charged with such offenses as contempt of court and bilking trusting clients, or consorting with known criminals. It has been further reinforced by all the undue attention given to attorneys who have become targets of investigations after successfully running for high (or even the highest) office.

And speaking of the latter, it is only when we stop to realize just how many of our top politicians possess law degrees that we can truly appreciate the potential consequences of such overt discrimination. For should the idea of closing entire neighborhoods to lawyers catch on, we may soon find ourselves living in a society truly divided between leaders and followers, with the former largely segregated into their own gated ghettos of law-school graduates and thus having even less identification and interaction with everyday working folks than they already do.

That's why it's about time we finally put aside our prejudices toward those who seem different merely because they have a license to practice law, access to the courts and the right to realize substantial (if not huge) gains from other people's losses.

And if that's not enough to get you to stop laughing at those lawyer jokes, all I can tell you, chum, is this: The next time you need legal advice, try calling a comedian.

FEAR FABRICATIONS

THERE'S NOTHING LIKE FEAR ITSELF TO SEE US THROUGH FEARFUL TIMES

(Originally published in The SandPaper, May 2009)

Assuming office at the height of the Great Depression, at a time when it appeared that America's economic system might not survive, an ebullient President Franklin D. Roosevelt buoyed up the nation by famously and fearlessly declaring that there was really "nothing to fear but fear itself."

But that was then. Today, as we contend with another major economic crisis, albeit one not quite as severe (not yet, anyway), fear is nothing if not a palpable and pervasive presence, forever keeping us on red alert for potential threats and menaces of every description that seem to pop up and down like the mini-monsters in some computer game.

And, lest we let down our guard for so much as a day, a fearsome force of fear-mongers stands ready to further feed our fears and amplify our anxiety levels by providing us with a steady flow of fear-inspiring fixations that attach themselves first to one thing and then another, fluctuating in intensity from week to week and month to month.

It wasn't all that long ago, for example, that we were being whipped into a frenzy of fear of undocumented immigrant laborers by a shrill, self-styled cable-network cabal of contemporary Paul Reveres. Allowing this wave of "illegal aliens" to sneak into the country to steal our unskilled jobs and help themselves to our society's many supposed benefits, so the warnings went, would ultimately bring about the corrosion of our culture and the languishing of our language. It therefore was incumbent on us to use any means possible—walls, posses, mass arrests and deportations and perhaps even a baseball bat or two upside the head—to make them feel distinctly unwelcome.

But then a funny thing happened—the menacing Mexican migrants at issue largely halted their northward movement, probably due as much to this country's curtailment of employment opportunities as to the inhospitable reception. And not a moment too soon, because had they not, they would no doubt have been blamed for the spread of a far more terrifying threat from south of the border that had quite suddenly catapulted into the No. 1 spot on our greatest fears list. And that, of course, was the new strain of flu we were given official instructions to refer to, as "H1N1" for fear that calling it "swine flu" would negatively impact the nation's pork processors, who were in all probability responsible for giving rise to it by substituting porcine concentration camps for traditional pigpens.

Instead, people visiting Mexico on tourist visas, including students on spring break, were said to have been inadvertently responsible for the pandemic panic into which the outbreak quickly mutated. But when it soon became apparent that this particular flu strain had lost most of its punch, despite its continued capacity to land a lethal one every now and then, our immediate fear subsided, or at least went into a dormant state while we all wait to see if it re-emerges next winter in a far more fearful formulation (enabling vaccine manufacturers to score another big bonanza in the meantime).

However, a new prospective peril was once again causing our apprehension level to appreciate appreciably. Should President Obama actually fulfill his promise to close down the U.S. military lockup for prisoners of the war on terror at Guantanamo Bay, might some or all its 240 remaining inmates somehow end up here in our very midst? It was a possibility, however remote, that Americans found so unnerving that the president's request for funding to facilitate the shutdown was roundly rejected by practically the entire Senate.

After all, since we had so often been reassured that the Gitmo detainees were "the worst of the worst," then these particular prisoners, who were still there after more than twice their number had already been sent home, must be nothing less than the worst of the worst of the worst. In fact, these dudes were probably so determined to do us harm that no amount of enhanced interrogation could cause them to crack. Would even the most maximal of our maximum-security prisons be capable of containing these jihadists Hannibal Lecters? Then again, the fact that there was no evidence against most of them that would hold up in a legitimate court of law made it appear even likelier that they'd walk—and want to take revenge on the first Americans they encountered for their years of unindicted incarceration.

But really, who needs to be concerned with the mere possibility that suspected terrorists may be freed to roam our streets when they're probably already roaming the aisles of our supermarkets? Or at least that seems to be the message conveyed—every couple minutes or so—on the closed circuit TV that sits just above the fruit bins at our local Acme.

"If you suspect it, report it!" admonishes a stern, Orwellian female voice punctuating the screen's ongoing purchasing suggestions and food-preparation tips. Then the disembodied voice, accompanied by fast-moving images, including one of a person peering through binoculars, goes on to advise us of the things we should be sure and report: "Packages left unattended," "people who seem out of place," and in general, "any suspicious activity," before concluding that "our most effective weapon against terrorism is you" and providing us with a state government hot-line number to call.

If people who seem out of place may actually be terrorists lurking in our own metaphorical back yard, however, there's something that's apt to be growing in our actual back yards—and even worse, on our front lawns—that may seem not just out of place to many a homeowner, but perhaps even more terrifying than a terrorist when left unattended.

I'm referring, of course, to the dreaded dandelion.

What is it, you might ask, that makes this quite edible and indeed nutritious plant such an object of fear and loathing that people will gladly resort to toxic chemical weapons to eradicate it from their yards? How could a cheery little yellow flower that helps provide pollen and nectar for honeybees fill men's hearts with such acrimony and alarm as to inspire one lawn care franchise to actually declare a "dandelion war"?

It was a phenomenon that I myself found a bit baffling until a supposed homeowner appearing in a television commercial clarified

REPEAT OFFENDERS

it for me. As he explained it, the very presence of dandelions on his lawn had put his family in imminent peril of being shunned and ostracized. The aura of disfavor and disgrace seemed to dissipate, however, once they made their premises dandelion free. "Neighbors smile when they see us now," he declared with obvious relief.

At last I understood: Dandelions, it seems, are the illegal aliens of flowering plants, as much to be feared for the threat they pose to the safe, monochromatic nature of our suburban culture as were people of color a few decades ago.

But that's what's so reassuring about consternation—it's the one commodity we can rely on to keep assuming new and novel forms if not giving new life to older ones, and thus remain profitable even when times are tough. Whether reflected in how we make our laws or how we mange our lawns, and whether cultivated by a Dick Cheney, a Glenn Beck or a hireling for a herbicide manufacturer, it's a sure bet that the only thing we need not fear will disappear is fear itself.

POSTAL PARANOIA: RETHINKING WHAT IS AND IS NOT A 'SUSPECT PIECE OF MAIL'

(Originally published in The SandPaper, November 2001)

Author's note: Return with me now to those frightening days following 9/11 when the U.S. mail became an object of fear and loathing—the result of what federal investigators now believe to have been a deranged government scientist 'going postal' by sending anthrax-laced letters to various prominent Americans in media and politics, as well as a major publisher of supermarket tabloids. While the episode, which killed five people and sickened 17 others, in addition to closing down a major postal facility, was certainly no joke, the response of the Postal Service, in a way, was.

Back in the early days of "Saturday Night Live" (when the show was actually funny), comedian Chevy Chase would regularly introduce the satirical Weekend Update segment with the words, "I'm Chevy Chase—and you're not."

Given current levels of fear and loathing of anthrax in the mail, that's just the sort of perspective that's needed to restore some measure of rationality to our lives today. Because in all probability, you're not Tom Brokaw, either—or Tom Daschle, Patrick Leahy, Dan Rather, Peter Jennings, George W. Bush, or any one of a number of other high-profile individuals who might conceivably be on the receiving end of a piece of contaminated or contagious correspondence.

You're also unlikely to be employed as a personal assistant to one of these luminaries. And while there's a somewhat better chance that you work for a major news organization or even a supermarket tabloid, even that's a statistical long shot.

What is extremely likely, however, is that you're recently received a card from the U.S. Postal Service with instructions on how to spot and handle a "suspect" piece of mail, millions of such cards having reportedly been sent out to the addresses it serves.

While it's comforting to know that our "security and peace of mind are paramount" to the service, according to an accompanying message from the postmaster general, it's this particular card itself that's more my idea of what a suspect piece of mail looks like.

That's because the one thing that postal officials have been unable to assure us of is that any item processed in their facilities hasn't been cross contaminated by potentially deadly anthrax spores, that apparently were spread through the system by a few letters sent to some of the above-named figures (along with at least one major newspaper and a large publisher of supermarket tabloids).

To the best of my knowledge, however (and apparently that of investigators), none of us "ordinary" citizens has yet been the personal recipient of any letters deliberately laced with anthrax.

Thus, despite the Postal Service's warnings, I must admit that getting mail from someone I don't know, or that's handwritten or has no return address, or bears "excessive postage" or lots of tape is not something I would find particularly alarming (especially since my family maintains a web site that invites letters and drawings from children). Nor am I concerned about any missives that might be addressed to a previous occupant (which we get all the time), that are lopsided or lumpy, or marked "personal" or "confidential" (terms that junk mailers are especially fond of using).

And I'm especially not inclined to want to "notify local law enforcement authorities" (per the Postal Service's recommendations) should mail matching any of these descriptions arrive at our box, being of the opinion that they have far more pressing matters to attend to.

But what I am currently concerned about are all envelopes, which I now make a habit of immediately discarding, as well as magazines whose covers I now feel inclined to wipe clean with antiseptic (In fact, what I'd ideally like to see are more periodicals, catalogues and the like mailed out in plastic bags). Oh, and post cards—like the ones being mailed out by the folks at the Postal Service, which I also can't help feeling may pose a pathogenic hazard.

And that's how I, for one, plan to go on treating the mail—at least, until I can be provided some reasonable assurance that the distribution facilities have been given a clean bill of health (particularly here in New Jersey, where the malevolent missives supposedly originated), and, hopefully, the perpetrator or perpetrators of this postal pestilence are apprehended.

Not that this doesn't have it's own drawbacks, however. Discarding the envelopes that correspondence, bills and the like came in, for instance, tends to create even more disorganization than is routine for our household.

And my decontamination efforts haven't been without their share of human error. On one recent occasion, for instance, I accidentally threw out the bag containing the mail itself, rather than the suspect envelopes, and had to retrieve it from the Dumpster.

Then there was the incident in which I casually mentioned to a convenience store deli clerk that those disposable plastic gloves she was wearing would be perfect for collecting mail from our post office box, prompting her to actually offer me a pair. After using them, however, I was somewhat startled to discover both my hands coated with a white powder (which turned out, fortunately, to be a harmless variety used to make it easier to slip the gloves on). Some might even say that's what comes of being overly cautious.

But one thing I feel reasonably sure of is that, since I'm neither a big-name personality nor in the employ of some highly influential institution, no terrorist, whether foreign or domestic, would be inclined to single me out for a personal germ-warfare attack.

Just in case I'm wrong, however, I've informed the editors of this publication that if any envelopes should arrive at their office after this column appears with requests to forward them to me (whether or not they be handwritten, lumpy or bearing excessive postage), I'd really rather they be returned to sender.

Author's note: In the spring of 2013, more than a decade after the 'anthrax attack' following 9/11, letters laced with traces of the deadly nerve agent ricin were mailed to President Obama and New York City Mayor Michael

REPEAT OFFENDERS

Bloomberg. Following the mistaken arrest of a Mississippi Elvis impersonator, the missives were eventually traced to (of all people) a Texas TV actress. The suspect, who had appeared in "The Vampire Diaries" and "The Walking Dead," initially told authorities her husband was the responsible party but ended up being charged herself in a reported attempt to frame him. So while in the 2001 episode, a supermarket tabloid publisher was among the targets, this more recent incident reads more like something one might only expect to find in...a supermarket tabloid.

ALMANAC ALERT: ONE SMALL STEP FROM SATIRE

(Originally published in The Philadelphia Inquirer, January 2004)

A couple of weeks ago, I e-mailed a story from *The Onion* to a friend who was unfamiliar with the satirical paper. In response, she queried, "Is this for real?"

No, I replied, it was simply an inspired send-up of current events that, in typical *Onion* fashion, had been contrived to sound exactly like a genuine article.

But in these strange times, it's becoming harder and harder to distinguish between what's factual and what's facetious.

While online the other night, for instance, I chanced upon an item that I thought worth reading aloud, prompting my sister to comment, "You must be looking at *The Onion* again."

"No," I replied. "This actually appears to be from the Associated Press." But I could well understand my sister's reaction. There is, after all, something distinctly "Onionesque" about the headline "FBI issues alert against almanac carriers" and the accompanying article, which stated in part:

"In a bulletin sent Christmas Eve to about 18,000 police organizations, the FBI said terrorists may use almanacs 'to assist with target selection and pre-operational planning.' It urged officers to watch during searches, traffic stops and other investigations for anyone carrying almanacs, especially if the books are annotated in suspicious ways."

And just how did almanacs suddenly come to be included among the tools of the terrorism trade?

According to the FBI, their contents typically include "profiles of cities and states and information about waterways, bridges, dams, reservoirs, tunnels, buildings and landmarks," often accompanied by photographs and maps. All of which would be consistent with "known methods of al-Qaeda and other terrorist organizations that seek to maximize the likelihood of operational success through careful planning." The Associated Press has confirmed the authenticity of the warning.

Allow me to offer two theories for your consideration.

The first is in the truth-is-stranger-than-fiction category: The feds have concluded that, where terrorist activity is concerned, a little knowledge is indeed a dangerous thing.

Now, admittedly, this may seem like an odd evaluation of the modus operandi of a group capable of planning anything as complex and well coordinated as the Sept. 11 attacks.

But it begins to make more sense when you stop and think that the current occupant of the Oval Office requires only cursory comprehension of the day's events to plan how this country's affairs and strategies will be conducted. President Bush readily admits that he never bothers reading newspapers (beyond, say, a quick scan of the headlines), relying instead on information from underlings he thinks might be taking the actual time to read them.

And if so little knowledge is required for the making of top-level decisions in the most powerful nation on Earth, why should we assume the terrorists need to rely on any source of information more sophisticated than an almanac to "carefully plan" their dastardly deeds? Viewed from that perspective, the story gains credibility (and also raises the possibility they might be turning to *The Old Farmer's Almanac* to plan attacks on rural areas).

My other theory, however, is that when people who consult almanacs are supposedly suspect, so is the news itself.

Remember the Office of Strategic Influence, the Pentagon disinformation agency that was supposed to have been officially closed up in 2002? I think this latest warning could be a sign that it's alive and well, as busy as ever concocting cockamamie news stories.

Only in this case, it's being done with a domestic target in mind— the aforementioned *Onion*, whose lampoonery has consistently mocked government policies (claiming, for example, that the Patriot Act was being expanded to make it illegal to read the Patriot Act).

What better way to put these put-on artists out of circulation than by planting in the media supposedly legitimate articles that blur the distinction between reality and ridicule?

I'll leave it to you to decide which of those theories seems more plausible. But, just to be on the safe side, as long as terrorism continues to be a threat, I'd advise you to think seriously about leaving your almanac at home. Especially if it's annotated in any way that might arouse suspicions that it could be used to facilitate an almanac attack.

OBJECTS OF MY OBJECTION

TAKING THE OFFENSIVE

(Originally published in the Berkshire Eagle, June 1994)

While I fully realize that it's no longer considered anything to brag about, there's no getting around the fact that I wasn't born yesterday. I'll even admit to being old enough (albeit just barely) to remember the time that a joking reference to a (gasp!) "water closet" was considered so controversial as to summon forth a network censor, thus precipitating a certain late-night talk show host's abrupt (if temporary) departure from the air.

How must Jack Paar be reacting these days, I wonder, to prime-time bathroom-humor sequences that depict people actually sitting in water closets (although, thankfully, with the stall doors closed), the gag being a shortage of toilet paper—or to a sitcom scene focusing on a woman's reaction to the size of a man's sex organs upon accidentally encountering him in the nude.

As for my own reaction, however, I'm willing to come right out and say that I find the airing of such coarseness under the guise of comedy offensive—and to further opine that anyone who doesn't either (1) was born yesterday and simply doesn't know any better, or (2) has a water closet for a brain. And if that offends you, well, frankly, I don't give a damn.

In fact, I think it's safe to say that America has become a country full of insensitive tube boobs who, culturally speaking, no longer know their elbow from their arschloch.

It's safe to say, that is, because this is still America and not Germany.

If it were Germany, I could be charged with a criminal offense and made to pay a hefty fine for directing such insolence at my countrymen. There, the use of terms such as "arschloch" (which I'll be tasteful enough not to translate for you, even though a great metropolitan newspaper recently did), are expressly verboten under a law that defines insult as "the illegal attack on the honor of another person through international expression of disrespect."

In America, by contrast, thanks in no small measure to the decline in censorship and general standards of decorum, you and I are free to be as intentionally disrespectful as we please—even to the point of calling somebody we don't like the English translation of an arschloch—provided that we keep such imprecations confined within certain boundaries.

Here, when such displays of incivility get us into trouble, it's usually because we haven't been paying enough attention to where those boundaries lie.

A good example is the trouble you can get into once having entered a jai alai fronton in the state of Connecticut. Generally at such establishments, it's considered entirely permissible for patrons to hurl any type of expletive at the players that enter their heads. One can scream expressions of disrespect for a contender's athletic ability, manhood, honor, or even his mother, and not expect a word of reprimand. But use anything that can be remotely construed as "abusive language" to a security guard or fronton official, and you can be placed on a lengthy list of "undesirables" and permanently barred from all state-supervised gaming facilities (as has happened to some perfectly desirable individuals with whom I'm acquainted).

In other cases, you need not be either insulting or abusive, but merely critical to find yourself in hot water. A rule of a New Jersey senior community, for example, specifies that "no owner, guest or lessee is authorized to direct or to reprimand any employee of the development," with violators subject to a $50 fine.

Nor does the object of criticism even have to be a person, various state legislatures now having made it an offense to insult certain commodities. Under a Florida law, for instance, one can be sued for publicly insinuating that a fruit or vegetable grown in the state is unsafe to eat without having scientific evidence to that effect.

It's also possible to transgress simply because you're unaware that someone has changed the rules of the game—like the game of Scrabble, for instance.

Until very recently, Scrabble represented the ultimate in recreational freedom of expression—a form of intellectual competition in which no word, no matter how arcane or vulgar, couldn't be invoked and positioned in such a manner as to jack up the score of a clever or articulate player. All that mattered was that the word in question was included in the official Scrabble Players Dictionary—a comprehensive volume that clearly noted when any such entry was considered an "offensive term."

But no more, for it seems that such language is now in the process of being purged from that all-inclusive lexicon, with some 50 to 100 words "deemed potentially offensive to people on the basis of religion, race, ethnicity, sex or sexual orientation" due for deletion. Never mind that some familiar ethnic slur or sexist expression may represent the only means of getting that crucial eight-point letter counted twice on a game-winning triple-letter-score square. Don't even think about spelling it out, not even in the privacy of your own living room in the company of close friends or family members, lest you make a miniscule contribution to the remote danger of America's becoming anything like what Germany used to be.

Such extremes of newfound political correctness, however, merely succeed in insulting our intelligence while failing utterly to compensate for the decline and fall of simple, old-fashioned politeness. If we really want to entertain the idea of creating a less offensive society, perhaps a better starting point would be with the insult to our remaining sense of propriety and civility that has increasingly come to pass for entertainment.

Authors note: Since this essay was first published, Connecticut's jai alai frontons all closed down due to a decline in patronage (perhaps helped along by the many regular patrons permanently banned), and the one from which the individuals of my acquaintance were ejected has been torn down to boot. And Jack Paar, sadly, passed on in 2004 without giving his reaction (at least that I'm aware of) to the proliferation of toilet humor and other daily descents into lewdness on TV (even as the Federal Communications Commission levies fines against networks for so-called "wardrobe malfunctions" during live telecasts).

IF THIS IS 'NEWS', THAT SURE IS NEWS TO ME

(Originally published in The SandPaper, August 2006)

Recently, a juxtaposition occurred on the "NBC Nightly News" that could just as easily have been part of the "Weekend Update" newscast lampoon regularly aired by the same network on "Saturday Night Live."

First came a segment dedicated to e-mails from viewers who found fault with the broadcast's coverage. One considered it too pro-Israel, another too anti-Israel, while a third thought the Iraq war was being given short shrift. In addressing the latter complaint, anchor Brian Williams explained that there was only so much in the complex course of daily events that could be covered in a 30-minute news program (that included commercials).

Having said that, he proceeded to the final item on the evening's agenda—a three-minute-long examination of whether repetition of the slogan in a headache remedy commercial, "HeadOn: apply directly to the forehead," was so incredibly annoying as to be highly effective.

Upon viewing that somewhat frivolous finale, I was almost inclined to send him an e-mail myself. It would have repeated a phrase used in another TV ad, this one for a state lottery, in which a young man excitedly reveals to a family gathering that his girlfriend has just cut her hair, prompting the announcer to respond, "that's not news."

Or perhaps I should say that if the reaction of the viewing public to a neo-hypnotic sales pitch belongs in the realm of real-world events and issues—especially with so much going on and so little space available to report it—that sure is news to me.

But such thinly disguised catering to commercial interests is only a small part of the problem of a media industry that devotes far too much emphasis to "news" that is either nonessential or downright nonsensical.

REPEAT OFFENDERS

A typical example of the former is the recent media frenzy over what movie star Mel Gibson is reported to have said following his arrest for driving under the influence. In addition to the coverage it received on standard news broadcasts, hours of airtime on cable outlets such as MSNBC were dedicated to the drunken, anti-Semitic tirade in which he apparently engaged, and to his subsequent contrition.

Now, I'm not saying the episode wasn't red meat for tabloids, gossip columnists and their televised equivalents, or that the late-night comics weren't justified in milking Mel for all he was worth. But Gibson, it should be remembered, is an actor and director, not a policy maker—and unless he should attempt to follow in the footsteps of Ronald Reagan, his intoxicated invective really didn't merit anything like the kind of sustained coverage it generated.

But while the Gibson affair might have had some legitimate news value, the same can't really be said of all the attention lavished on "flag desecration"—about as frivolous an issue as the campaign to clothe animals that elicited so much coverage (and so many contributions) back in the 1950s before being exposed as the work of a professional prankster.

News executives, of course, might attempt to justify the exaggerated coverage of such marginal concerns by pointing out that their product, like those of its advertisers, is a commodity, and that they are simply responding to the interests of its target audience. That may be true, but it's also true that by focusing so much of the spotlight on sideshows and illusions, when not shining it on conflict, crime and cataclysm, the news media are actually cheating their consumers out of information that they really need to know.

A good illustration is something that occurred earlier this month—an event that you probably didn't see, hear or read about, but that could have profound implications for your family's health and well-being. I'm taking about the arrival of the August 3 deadline for the Environmental Protection Agency's decade-long review of the safety of all pesticides that was mandated under the Food Quality Protection Act or FQPA, the "peace of mind guarantee" that was signed into law in 1996 by President Clinton.

This massive reassessment, the stated purpose of which was to establish "reasonable certainty that no harm will result to infants and children from aggregate (meaning multi-source) exposure" to any particular pesticide, was, in fact, the subject of two cursory press releases issued by the EPA Newsroom at the beginning of the month, which cite restrictions on or cancellations of a handful of the more than 1,100 pesticides covered.

Neither release specifically mentioned infants or children. The first, however, attributed to EPA Administrator Stephen L. Johnson the statement that "The Bush Administration is ensuring pesticides used to grow the fruits, vegetables and other foods families are serving meet the highest protective standards in the world." In the second one, Johnson was further quoted as crediting both the EPA and the administration with "maintaining the highest ethical and scientific standards" in carrying out the task, and as having thereby "planted the seeds to yield healthier lives for generations of American families."

Reading such self-congratulatory declarations may well create an impression that the lack of coverage is merely another case of the liberal media overlooking the positive achievements of the Bush Administration. But what actually took place, and was under-reported to the extent that most Americans were probably unaware of it, is a story of a far different nature.

I'm referring to an event at the end of May when, in anticipation of the deadline, the heads of the EPA unions representing some 9000 staff scientists sent an open letter to Johnson accusing EPA officials of bowing to industry pressure and leaving Americans, especially children, vulnerable to the toxic effects of the pesticides supposedly being reevaluated. "We are concerned that the Agency has not, consistent with its principles of scientific integrity and sound science, adequately summarized or drawn conclusions about the developmental neurotoxicity data received from pesticide registrants," reads one paragraph. "Our colleagues within the Agency, including EPA's Inspector general, believe it would be premature to conclude that there is a complete and reliable database…upon which to base any final tolerance reassessment decisions as required by the FQPA."

REPEAT OFFENDERS

Now that *is* news—or should have been.

"The fact that this letter had to be sent at all is an utter disgrace," declared Jeff Ruch, Executive Director of Public Employees for Environmental Responsibility (PEER). But "even more disgraceful," he added, "is the likelihood that this warning will be disregarded by an agency that is supposed to be protecting public health and the environment."

Perhaps the ultimate disgrace, however, is the fact that what ought to be a burning issue in this country—its apparent willingness to sacrifice the health and safety of its children on the alter of industry profits—has been mostly disregarded by the media in favor of a fabricated flap over flag burning. Or that the sobering concerns voiced by thousands of government scientists should not only be blithely disregarded by the people in power, but should have to take a back seat to the drunken rant of a bigoted movie actor.

It's enough to make me want to stop saying no to drugs just long enough to procure some of that HeadOn and apply it directly to my forehead.

Author's note: Not much seems to have changed in the nature of television journalism since this essay was first published. Frivolous items continue to consume valuable airtime. And vitally important issues that affect everyone, such as the initiatives in various states to pass legislation requiring the labeling of genetically engineered food (something done in more than five dozen other countries) and attempts in Congress to superseded such efforts, have at this writing received little or no coverage. (But then, what can one expect when so many advertising dollars are spent promoting those foods, as well as the herbicide Roundup, which is also sprayed on genetically altered crops?)

A BLOW TO AN EGALITARIAN EGO

(Originally published in the Orlando Sentinel, January 1998)

Ever since college, when the faculty sponsor of our campus newspaper took to referring to me as its "crusading editor," I have fancied myself a steadfast supporter of the underprivileged and downtrodden.

It has therefore come as something of a shock to discover that I have been operating under a mere delusion of compassion and that, however I may have disguised them to myself and others, my true sympathies lay with an "elite minority" of oppressors of the working poor.

Being made so acutely aware of my own ethical shortcomings has been, I admit, a humbling experience, especially because I'm not sure I have what it takes to rise above them. But I can do the next most honorable thing, which is to confess the full extent of my intolerance toward something considered so vital to a group of exploited, largely immigrant laborers that saving it has become the goal of a full-fledged hunger strike.

I'm referring to that gasoline-powered gardening gadget commonly known as the leaf blower.

Yes, I'll own up to having harbored a distinct bias—an actual hatred, in fact—toward this deafening device ever since one first came within earshot of my residence and made me want to do some blowing away myself (an impulse kept in check only by my prudent reluctance to keep a firearm handy). Little did I realize, however, how counterproductive such an attitude actually was. In fact, my hypocrisy in this regard well might never have intruded on my misconceived liberal sensibilities had I not learned about a recent decision of the Los Angeles City Council to ban the use of leaf blowers, and the extent of the resulting sound and fury.

For though it may look and sound like nothing more than an air-agitating apparatus of dubious necessity, the leaf blower has turned out to be a source of even greater turbulence in the political landscape than in the residential one.

What's at issue is the negative impact that a return to the repressiveness of the rake will have on the meager incomes of those charged with maintaining the appearance of the green, green grass of home for the average affluent Angeleno.

According to Adrian Alvarez, an artist who serves as spokesman for a group of Hispanic gardeners organized to fight the ban, the leaf blower is what enables its members—who are paid as little as $70 a month for weekly service calls—to tackle a dozen or more yards daily.

Alvarez, one of 11 people protesting the edict via a hunger strike, acknowledged that "leaf blowers make noise," but decried the ordinance as one "exclusively designed to address the concerns of an elite minority of residents."

To me, an ardent admirer of the late Cesar Chavez (whose hand I once shook) and his hunger strikes on behalf of maltreated migrant farm workers, Alvarez's words came as a stinging rebuke. Had I really sunk so low as to identify with those privileged classes who would ruthlessly rob the poor of the few paltry prerogatives left to them?

How would I feel, after all, if a ban were to be placed on word processors, forcing me to go back to having to type and retype my manuscripts the old-fashioned way?

But then, my word processor isn't something that obliterates all other forms of auditory stimuli such as conversation (not to mention concentration). And it doesn't pollute the environment with noxious fumes. So, as low-minded as it might seem, I'm afraid I'm going to have to let my composure, rather than my conscience, be my guide in this particular matter—and if that means sleeping with the enemies of equity, at least the noise won't keep me awake.

Not that the proponents of leaf-blowing need any support from me or my ill-disposed ilk, having far more powerful allies in their corner, such as the makers of the equipment themselves who have filed suit to have the ban lifted. Perhaps the nation's over-the-counter drug manufacturers might even be persuaded to come to their defense, given the substantial boost the devices have undoubtedly contributed to the overall sales of headache remedies.

But however they come to be accepted, I expect to go on passively resisting these infernal instruments wherever I encounter them, believing leaves are best left wherever the wind blows them—and being ready to absorb whatever additional blows to my egalitarian ego that might result.

Author's note: While the word processor referred to here may now have become as outmoded as "having to type and retype my manuscripts the old-fashioned way," the leaf blower, unfortunately has remained every bit as noisy, polluting and infuriating as it was back when this was written. It's also perhaps a bit ironical—and an indication of the perverse nature of the Internet—that ads for leaf blowers can be found accompanying this op-ed essay in the article archives of The Orlando Sentinel.

SUMMERTIME BLUES—AN UNDERRATED MALADY

(Originally published in The SandPaper, October 1993)

"Read this," my sister instructed me as she plunked a copy of the magazine *Organic Gardening* down on the desk where I was working one recent brisk autumn evening. "These are my sentiments exactly."

The item with which she was so in accord turned out to be a "Letter from California" by contributing editor Jeff Cox. It told how when he had lived back East, he had regarded fall as a "tragic time" of the year that evoked a "poignant mixture of melancholy, nostalgia and dread," along with the prospect of "lonely, threatening, frozen days and never-ending nights." Contrasting with such dreary reminiscences were the joys of growing winter flowers and crops in his present locale.

If the thought was eloquently expressed, the theme was an all-too-familiar one. Indeed, the chilly reception that the dipping of the mercury is given in many quarters at this time of year is amply evident in everything from the commercials for tropical getaways to the annual appearance of all those newspaper articles about the "winter blahs" and actual depression suffered by many the minute sunlight starts to diminish.

The problem, as I see it, is that those whose spirits fall along with the leaves have been monopolizing the propaganda market, while the rest of us who, like myself, have the reverse reaction to seasonal change are compelled to suffer summer after summer in stifling silence.

That's why I now feel it necessary to assume the role of spokes-man for my largely unacknowledged segment of society, the thermally challenged, in order to put our hatred of heat on a par with the teeth-chattering crowd's fear of frigidity.

It's not that individuals such as ourselves are incapable of taking delight, just as they do, in sweet springtime's aesthetic beauties—it's just that such pleasures are overshadowed for us by the knowledge of the oppressive three-to-four month ordeal this primrose path inevitably leads up to. It's probably quite a bit akin, in fact, to the way they feel about the majestic hues of autumn.

I'll concede that it may be difficult for some of them to comprehend how anybody besides, say, a dedicated winter-sports enthusiast (which I, for one, am not) could possibly prefer January to June, or find anything less than agreeable about August.

Let's just say that some of us—a considerable number, I would suspect—aren't made particularly happy by the sensation of sunshine on our shoulder, or on any part of our epidermis, for that matter. We could no more conceive of letting ourselves "bask" for hours on a beach chair in 90-degree-plus temperatures than they could think in terms of spending a below-zero morning engaged in ice fishing.

In fact, we'd generally prefer to be outdoors as little as possible during those lazy, hazy, crazy days of scorching rays, inverted air and oppressive ozone levels. This makes us, in effect, summertime shut-ins, largely exiled to air-conditioned confinement (if we're lucky enough to have air conditioning) while our cold-blooded compatriots are out on the jogging track or tennis court.

And what happens when we do occasionally attempt to seek relief from such "cabin fever" by venturing outside on some relatively cool day or evening? Invariably, if the skeeters (or gnats, or greenheads) don't get us, the pesticides will—whether drifting in our direction from someone's chemically permeated property down the street or rendering us part of the "collateral damage" of an airborne assault.

Then, too, even allowing for those cooler air masses that may now and then bring some small measure of relief from summer swelter, weather-wise it tends to be an abysmally boring season. Hence, the physical torpor this torrid time produces is apt to be compounded by a creeping psychological one as well. As an old rock 'n roll song so aptly put it, "there ain't no cure for the summertime blues"—provided, of course, that you're among those of us who are prone to them.

But if we can somehow manage to survive the dog days, the pollution levels, the pests, the pesticides and the sheer ennui of it all, there comes a time when the days become shorter and less oppressive. The nights get chillier, and the bugs all gradually begin disappearing from the scene, along with the bug sprays. Then, in a truly miraculous turn of events, the trees go from dull green to lively, brilliant shades of red and orange, and the air becomes brisk, clean and alive with the joy and excitement of approaching winter and its genuinely soul-stirring weather potentials.

In short, the season arrives when we climatically perverse people begin to snap out of our summer-long stupor and come back into our element. Our spirits are uplifted by every new day of plummeting temperatures and cascade of descending leaves, and our hearts warmed by each new frost and freeze warning on the evening weather report.

I could use any number of terms to describe the elation with which fall fills us summer-is-a-bummer types, but they wouldn't be any more eloquent than those used by Jeff Cox in his letter from California relating his feelings of "anticipation, exhilaration and renewal" at the prospect of fall as "transformed" by the Golden West.

Without the need for any such transformation, those describe my sentiments exactly.

Author's note: Two decades after this essay first appeared, New York Times columnist Frank Bruni indicated those were his sentiments as well by writing an anti-summer diatribe entitled "The meanest season." One response, published by the website The Blaze ran under the headline, "NYT columnist hates summer, may also hate children and butterflies." See what I mean?

MOST OF ALL, YOU'VE GOT TO HIDE IT FROM THE KIDS

(Originally published in The Philadelphia Inquirer, March 2002)

Before you proceed to read this out loud (if you're so inclined), I feel obliged to warn you that some of the material it contains may not be suitable for impressionable children, especially if they're Girl Scouts.

You may, of course, be curious to know what would prompt me to issue such a warning. Well, let's just say that having already been accused of making certain inappropriate remarks in the presence of Girl Scouts (and maybe even Brownies?), I thought it best to try to avoid giving similar offense while attempting to clarify what actually took place.

I recently had the indelicacy to suggest that at least one of the ingredients in Girl Scout Cookies might be hazardous to the health of those consuming them. It's not that I consider these good-intentioned goodies to be any worse than countless other processed-food products. But I do believe they have a self-imposed obligation to be somewhat better.

I might never have mentioned this with children present, however, had they not eagerly entreated me to buy one or more boxes of the cookies in question as I entered my local supermarket late one afternoon.

Thanks, but no thanks, I replied, after scrutinizing a couple of the boxes—a rejection I thought they shouldn't take personally, since the cookies are a purely institutional commodity produced by a commercial bakery in a distant city, rather than in some scout leader's kitchen.

However, an adult accompanying the group asked if I found something wrong with the product. And I responded by politely pointing out that the vegetable oils listed among the ingredients were described as "partially hydrogenated." Such oils, I patiently explained, are a major dietary source of trans-fatty acids, now generally acknowledged to be a culprit in the development of heart disease, the nation's number-one killer.

REPEAT OFFENDERS

My criticism was enough to elicit from this scout mother some of her own misgivings about junk food and bovine growth hormone in milk. I then suggested that it might behoove the Girl Scouts to market cookies with organic ingredients.

We were chatting in this manner when an unsmiling woman who seemed to rank higher in the Girl Scout hierarchy appeared and proceeded to throw cold water on the discussion.

After articulating her resentment at my having singled out Girl Scout cookies when the supermarket was so full of items with questionable ingredients, she went on to say I should take my concerns up with "the [Girl Scout] Council" and not voice them "in front of the children."

Then the woman with whom I had originally chatted followed me outside the store and, in a sudden and totally unexpected burst of indignation, declared, "How dare you do that to children!"

So in response, ladies, I'd like to quote from a piece of Girl Scout literature available on the Internet issued by the organization's Totem Council: "Lifestyle habits, especially eating and exercise behaviors, are established during childhood and are difficult to change in adulthood... Knowledge and healthy habits gained through Girl Scout programs can help girls make responsible decisions about their bodies that will benefit them for a lifetime."

Now, I can understand why some Girl Scout mothers might feel that they have to hide such concerns from the kids. A little knowledge, after all, can be a dangerous thing when possessed by children charged with the collective responsibility of unloading many thousands of boxes of cookies.

Some might even decide to simply quit the sales force until "the Council" decides to opt for ingredients that will help promote healthier lifestyle habits.

And that could well be the way these particular cookies crumble.

Author's note: Partially hydrogenated oil was still being listed as an ingredient in some Girl Scout Cookies (although not all varieties) nearly a decade after this column first appeared.

CULTURED PERILS

CONSUMER FRAUD OF THE 'VERSE' KIND

(Originally published in The SandPaper, April 1993)

A few years ago while lamenting about how the ravages of progress had brought about the progressive decline of various civilized institutions, I ventured an opinion that poetic license had actually degenerated into verse vice.

While fully aware of the risk of appearing to be enamored of one's own words (a peccadillo which should be reserved solely for poets), that particular observation is one I now believe should be the basis for a call to action of the kind that speaks louder than mere words.

What inspired this realization was a news item out of San Francisco—one having to do not so much with poetic license as poetic licensing, which a municipal code is said to require for the reading of so-called "poetry" in local coffee houses. Using a stepped-up enforcement of this 20-year-old decree, local authorities are now reportedly prevailing upon such establishments to obtain actual "entertainment permits" for said readings.

This demand has reportedly prompted Mayor Frank Jordan to fire off a letter of protest, which noted that "free speech is as important to San Francisco as the fog"—an analogy I thought was pretty good, considering that the kind of free speech to which the mayor was referring is usually about as clear as a San Francisco fog.

Whether the speech involved constitutes entertainment is another matter entirely. I suppose it would all depend on just how entertaining the patrons of the coffeehouses in question find this sort of discourse.

Speaking as someone who writes for a living, I have the same feeling about free speech in general as your typical National Rifle Association member does about his arsenal—once they require a permit, anything you might have to say is in jeopardy of being regulated.

That some regulation of our right to self-expression is in order, however, I have no doubt, and this is what I'm referring to when I speak of "verse vice." Specifically, I would like to see the authorities start clamping down on a steadily growing variety of cultural con artistry in the same way they now deal with the fraudulent misrepresentation of consumer products.

In essence, it is my belief that people should be allowed to express themselves in any way they please, but should be expressly prohibited from calling such self-expression anything they want.

Rap, for instance, ought not to be censored in any manner as long as it is simply referred to as "rap." But under no circumstances should it be permitted to go under such designations as "rap music" or "rap songs," "music" and "song" being labels whose use should be confined only to entities containing recognizable elements of melody and harmony.

Similarly, pornography ought to have no restrictions placed on its content, other than those relating to the age of the participants. But it also should not be allowed within, say, 500 feet of any art museum or gallery. (As for how we are to determine what constitutes pornography as opposed to art, I'll invoke an utterance once famously made by a Supreme Court justice to the effect that we'll know it when we see it.)

The fact is that by deliberately blurring the distinctions between sham and substance, we've succeeded in denigrating some of the most magnificent spheres of human achievement—but perhaps nowhere more so than in the realm of poetry.

One the exclusive domain of those with a genuine gift for working magic with words, poetry as both an art and a discipline has now been so completely hijacked by charlatans and imposters as to be rendered virtually unrecognizable—not to mention incomprehensible. From Pacific Coast coffeehouses to the pages of the *Atlantic Monthly*, there has continued to flow such a steady stream of gibberish, disconnected ramblings distinguished by neither rhyme nor reason, that a true poetic genius might today be inclined to disavow any association with the medium.

That's why restoring this once highest of art forms to its former glory calls for a drastic redefinition of what qualifies as genuine poetry and what doesn't. Admittedly, the reintroduction of standards for verifying the validity of verse won't be an easy undertaking at this late date. But it may be helpful to keep a few basic criteria in mind, such as: (1) meter, or something resembling it; (2) some sort of rhyme scheme (with, perhaps, an exemption for poets having a certain number of rhyming works to their credit; (3) some semblance of sense, and (4) some measure of aesthetics (which would pretty well disqualify any "rap poetry").

Most of all, the litmus test of a real poem should be whether it bears repeated recitation (by people other than its author) and is memorable enough to be worth memorizing.

As for those efforts that fail the test, there are all sorts of things we might call them: babble, double-talk, drivel, or perhaps even entertainment. But not poetry, for Keat's sake.

Let that "lordly name" be applied to them—nevermore!

A LONG RECORD OF LAMENTABLE LYRICS

(Originally published in The Berkshire Eagle and The SandPaper, July 1993)

Some years back, one of those briefly popular songs associated with one of those briefly popular dance crazes urged listeners to "blame it on the Bossa Nova."
Like so many numbers in the now-you-hear-them, now-you-don't category, that eminently forgettable song had remained safely locked up in my subconscious—that is, until its insistent lyrics were suddenly recalled to mind by the news of a murder trial playing out deep in the heart of Texas.

Not that anyone is claiming the Bossa Nova is to blame for the fatal shooting of a state trooper with which the defendant, Ronald Ray Howard, is charged. It's rather so-called "rap music" that's been made out to be the pop culture culprit in this case—the bad influence that Howard claims encouraged him to pull the trigger and helped to instigate his murderous attitude toward lawmen in general. As his lawyer told the court, "We think that he ought to be spared his life… due to the music."

The prosecutor, in fact, seemed to concur that rap should take at least part of the rap. The trooper's widow has gone so far as to file a product liability suit against Time Warner and one of the groups Howard was listening to just before her husband pulled over his stolen car for a missing headlight violation and was subsequently gunned down.

There can be no denying, of course, that the violent nature of some contemporary lyrics hasn't exactly been a soothing influence on the savage instincts lurking just below the surface of Western Civilization. And it seems quite plausible that many of the individuals engaging in antisocial behavior in recent years may have been at least somewhat emboldened by the message they convey.

REPEAT OFFENDERS

Now, it may be easy enough to dismiss such contemporary genres as something other than musical, Still, you must remember this: the lyrics of popular music have been a generally bad influence on society for many, many years. The fact is that long before the cacophonous cadences, threatening tones and ugly utterances that are so prevalent on today's airwaves, we were being lulled into all sorts of unbecoming conduct and undesirable attitudes by any number of seemingly pleasant, supposedly innocent and apparently harmless little tunes.

It may well be true, for instance, that the words to certain heavy metal songs have seduced some youthful listeners into attempting suicide. But in reflecting back on the romantic ballads of bygone days, we find suicidal suggestions galore—as in the notion that "life can't mean anything when your lover has gone," or in Al Jolson's even more direct assertion that he could "go right on living, or end it...it all depends on you."

Then, there have been allegations that some of today's so-called songs are demeaning to women and even have overtones of bondage. But just stop for a moment and consider the implications of the lyrics chirped by plucky, wholesome Teresa Brewer back around 1950: "I'd do anything for you, anything you'd want me to." Anything?

There are numerous examples, in fact, of the hit parades of years past having contributed heavily to male chauvinist attitudes, such as that old sentimental favorite advising men to "try a little tenderness" with their womenfolk, which the latter won't forget since "love is their whole happiness." Not to mention one of crooner Vaughn Monroe's biggest hits that berates a ballerina for forcing love to "wait its turn" while she goes on with her career, the result being that love is "gone, ballerina, gone," and all because she "wanted fame instead."

Or how about the decidedly unsubtle sexist suggestion that "You'll learn to cook and to sew / What's more, you'll love it I know / When you're a stay-at-home, play-at-home eight o'clock sleepy time gal."

Then again, if you think some of today's mega-hits encourage various forms of misconduct, the kind of behavior promoted by yesterday's charming vocals with instrumental accompaniment could be downright disorderly. One particular 1950s-era number, for example, urged those in the throes of infatuation to "wake the town and tell the people," even going so far as to "shout it from the highest steeple" and "ring the bells the whole night through." All of which could easily be construed as serious disturbances of the peace, to say nothing of breaking and entering.

While these may be mere misdemeanors, however, some of the actions encouraged by ballads of years gone by might currently get you charged with a felony. Such sentiments as Nat Cole's "I'll follow you my love, you'll never be free/to the ends of the earth, till you've given your love to me," or Eddie Fisher's "Though you may forget me, you're still on my mind/ Look over your shoulder, I'm walking behind" describe exactly the type of actions that could result in a good, stiff prison sentence under today's anti-stalking statutes.

And in retrospect, wasn't there something just a teeny bit unsavory about "The Children's Marching Song"? That particular anthem of the late '50s, if you're old enough to recall, featured a group of youngsters under the direction of Mitch Miller singing about an old man who played "knick-knack, paddy-whack" in an apparent interactive ritual with a child. Now really, would you want some old man from the neighborhood engaging in any such pastime with your kid?

Sure, it's easy enough to blame the stuff that now passes for popular music for many of the discordant notes in today's society and for everything that's out of tune with the times—especially when the medium involved has become the message and the message is often so blatantly menacing.

But clearly, the music industry's long-playing record of lamentable lyrics leaves a lot to be desired. And even though it's been a long, long time since tuneful and romantic melodies were in vogue, it's easy to remember just how many of those foolish things we used to say and do may have been a result of their not-so-subtle influence.

OVERKILLING A MOCKINGBIRD IN MUSKOGEE

(Originally published in The SandPaper, August 2001)

Back in the days when smoking pot was one of the ways that young people expressed their contempt for authority in general and the nation's policymakers in particular, a notable exception was the city of Muskogee, Oklahoma. Or at least it was in a song made popular by Merle Haggard, in which the country star vocalized the various reasons why he was "proud to be an Okie from Muskogee."

"We don't smoke marijuana in Muskogee," was one of those reasons. Which wasn't to say that folks there were necessarily models of law-abiding sobriety. For as the song went on to note, "white lightning's still the biggest thrill of all."

A literal interpretation of this '60s redneck anthem might thus be forced to conclude that down Muskogee way, it wasn't law but rather tradition that determined what constituted appropriate behavior. Smoking pot was a bad thing not because marijuana was an illegal substance per se, but because it was one favored by the anti-war, draft-card–burning hippies that the local good ol' boys held in such contempt, whereas the high produced by drinking moonshine whiskey was perfectly acceptable—even though it carried with it the risk of blindness.

If the song were written today, however, it might begin with something like, "We don't hurt people's feelings in Muskogee" and end by noting, "mutual respect's the biggest thing of all." Or at least, that's the impression one gets in trying to make sense of the local high school's having dispensed with a requirement that ninth graders read Harper Lee's Pulitzer Prize-winning novel *To Kill a Mockingbird*, the heartwarming tale of two siblings' experiences growing up in a small town in southern Alabama during the Great Depression.

What's a bit more difficult to understand is why this should have been news of national significance (had it not been, I wouldn't even have known about it). Or why the decision should be of any concern to the Oklahoma Civil Liberties Union, whose director, Joann Bell, reportedly has referred to it as "ludicrous."

It's not as though the school authorities in Muskogee had exactly banned the book, perhaps by banishing it from their library. It's just that it's no longer part of the freshman required reading program. That, according to Principal Terry Saul, consists of three of four works of classic literature, including Homer's *Odyssey* and Shakespeare's *Romeo and Juliet*, that are read and discussed in the classroom.

To Kill a Mockingbird was removed from that list, Saul was quoted as saying, because it contained "racially charged" language and "we didn't want to put any kids in an uncomfortable situation." The decision, the principal told me in a subsequent phone conversation, was made by "an administrative team" based on input from "students, teachers and people in the community."

As Dan Hattaway, an associate principal in charge of the ninth grade to whom Saul referred me, explained, "there were specific concerns from both the community and staff—enough of a concern to raise a red flag" about the wisdom of requiring that the book be read and discussed in a school system serving a population that's about 48 percent white, 25 percent black and 25 percent American Indian.

Not that either administrator denies that the book, in Saul's phrase, is a "meaningful, impactful" work that generates some powerful "life lessons"—the same kinds of lessons they'd like to impress on their students. It's just that in realigning the curriculum, he noted, "our mission is to try to build a climate of mutual respect for all kids," and "we just feel we can do it with other literature without the inappropriate language."

Or, as Hattaway put it, "If this in some way creates an avenue that creates hard feelings" or "generates a dialogue that's outside of (the novel's) framework" by "repeating bad words, is this the only work of literature we can use?"

Inappropriate language? Bad words? Having read *To Kill a Mockingbird* during my freshman year in college (as well as having seen the movie version at least two or three times), I was unable to recall any such offensive phraseology in this universally acclaimed 20th Century classic. So I leafed through a paperback copy to see if I had somehow missed something—and it was then that I realized what these seemingly well-intentioned Muskogee school officials were apparently referring to. It was the repeated occurrence of that dreaded, presently unspeakable "N" word—both in the way various characters talked about people of color and anyone suspected of "loving" them (in particular, the children's father, attorney Atticus Finch, when he unsuccessfully attempts to defend one such individual against a false sexual assault charge).

Such terminology, in fact, is actually addressed by Atticus in a couple of lectures to his 10-year-old daughter Scout. "Nigger-lover," he explains, is a term that "ignorant, trashy people use...when they think somebody's favoring Negroes over and above themselves. It's slipped into usage with some people like ourselves, when they want a common, ugly term to label somebody." (Here, it should be noted that "Negroes" an anachronistic term once in common usage, might also now be considered offensive, at least, according to my dictionary.)

"You aren't really a nigger-lover then, are you?" she asks, to which he replies, "I certainly am. I do my best to love everybody...it's never an insult to be called what somebody thinks is a bad name. It just shows you how poor that person is, it doesn't hurt you."

But it's one particular passage in the book, I believe, that really hits the nail on the head in explaining what it is that most concerns the folks in Muskogee—the one in which Atticus admonishes her, "Don't say nigger, Scout," to which she responds, "Well, if you don't want me to grow up talkin' that way, why do you send me to school?"

It's not the fact that students will be exposed to "bad words" per se, which, given the incredibly foul-mouthed climate of today's entertainment and media culture, even the most cloistered among them are bound to be subjected to. It's rather the possibility that the school system itself might in any way, shape or forum, be accused of exposing them to that "N" word, even when used within the context of an acknowledged literary masterpiece offering a telling perspective on the errors of our prejudicial ways.

In this respect, the language at issue, while it may be perfectly appropriate in terms of the time, place and people depicted, becomes "inappropriate" simply by virtue of being discussed by students in a classroom setting. Better to drop the book from the curriculum entirely rather than risk accusations that some guileless youth picked up the offending phrase from it—or worse yet, that some other youth was offended by its use there, no matter in what framework. (Apparently, however, this timidity about what might happen "outside the framework" of the assigned literature doesn't apply to another piece of required reading, *Romeo and Juliet*, in which the suicide of the star-crossed lovers is used to demonstrate the consequences that can result from a feud between families.)

All of which may indeed be "making a mountain out of a molehill," as Hattaway insisted. *To Kill a Mockingbird*, after all, is still available to any Muskogee high schoolers that wish to read it (and, as he pointed out to me, many more may now be motivated to do just that). Why, then, should its merely being no longer included in the ninth-grade curriculum generate any particular interest outside of the school district?

He does have a point, of course—perhaps this is a prime example of media overkill. But, by the same token, I think this seemingly insignificant local matter reflects a growing type of educational overkill as well—a disturbing trend that extends far beyond Muskogee. It's another manifestation of the "zero tolerance" principle at work—in this case, carrying nondiscrimination to the point where it renders meanings meaningless and makes no distinction between the benighted and the beneficial. It's the whole, bizarre notion that school authorities can somehow manage to control and sanitize the input that students receive in the same puritanical manner that they interpret innocuous medications as dangerous drugs, nail clippers as weapons, innocent stolen kisses as sexual harassment and harmless essays as criminal threats.

And while this particular issue may not have gotten anywhere near the point that calls for ACLU intervention, I do agree with the Oklahoma chapter's director that there is something ludicrous about it—that is, about the incongruity of trying to create an unreal and unreasonably insulated public-school environment in the midst of a culture awash in smut, obscenity, violent images and racial rancor.

It is every bit as ludicrous, say, as bragging about abstaining from marijuana while you're busy getting high on moonshine.

LAST WORDS ON MCVEIGH'S LAST WORDS

(Originally published in The SandPaper, June 2001)

When Alfred Hitchcock's cutting-edge horror film *Psycho* first hit neighborhood theaters back around 1960, it caused no small amount of consternation among people who suspected (correctly, as it turned out) that the previously restrained director of soft-core suspense had opened the cinematic shower door on a dark new genre of graphic gore—a door that would henceforth prove impossible to close.

Of course, there was no way that I as a teenager back then was going to pass up the chance to see the ultra-scary movie that everyone was talking about. And it certainly lived up to expectations, if the shrieks emitted by our small group of adolescents could be used as any sort of indicator.

But in the course of viewing the picture, I was bothered for an entirely different reason—an aspect of the film that I'd never seen alluded to in any subsequent references. What I found even more unsettling than the movie's macabre murder scenes was something one of the characters comes upon during a clandestine search of the living quarters of Norman Bates, the affable and accommodating motel manager with the criminally insane personality split.

It was a phonograph on which sat a recording of Beethoven's third symphony.

Right then, I knew Hitchcock had done his adopted country a major disservice. But worse than that, at least as far as I was personally concerned, he had in the stroke of a single camera shot stigmatized people such as myself who just naturally enjoyed listening to classical music. From now on, I remember thinking at the time, perhaps I'd better keep that particular proclivity to myself lest I be judged by my contemporaries (and perhaps even by my elders) as a potential homicidal maniac.

REPEAT OFFENDERS

Now, more than four decades after the initial conveying of that ever-so-subtle (in fact, nearly subliminal) message of lunacy-by-association to millions of Americans, it's happened again. Only this time, it involved a real-life case of criminal craziness—one whose final chapter managed to capture and mesmerize a far larger audience than any saga that either Hitchcock or anyone else in Hollywood could ever have orchestrated.

I'm talking about the coverage given the execution of Timothy McVeigh, the all-American soldier boy who managed to achieve a total body count of 168 of his countrymen (not to mention wounding a thousand or so more) with a homemade bomb.

Up to that point, it had never in fact occurred to me just how much of a resemblance this polite, sensitive-seeming and innocent-appearing young man bore to Norman Bates, who appeared (and thought himself) incapable of hurting a fly.

It is in their negative impact on our cultural climate, however, that I find the most disturbing similarity between the fictitious psychopath and the all-too-real one. And it was by executing the latter that we afforded him the opportunity to do some added damage, this time to the already flimsy foundation of America's artistic appreciation.

By that, I'm referring to McVeigh's invoking of 19th-century poet William Ernest Henley's *Invictus* to serve as a final statement.

Whether or not the Oklahoma City bomber had any right to identify with the sentiments in the verse (which some commentators, including the book editor of *The Philadelphia Inquirer*, have contended he didn't), is, I believe, far less important than the fact that he chose a poem in the first place to substitute for his "last words."

Perhaps it seems frivolous to raise such a point when talking about someone whose act ended so many lives and did such horrifying damage to so many others. But given the fact of there having been so much reported concern that McVeigh might use the occasion as an opportunity to further "hurt" the survivors in some way, I think it only appropriate to point out that his written statement was not nearly as innocuous as it may have seemed.

Its ripple effect, I fear, will be to push our society (in contrast to that of other civilized nations) even deeper into its aesthetic abyss by casting a cloud of suspicion on any tendency kids might show to savor and enjoy good verse. No such stigma, mind you, need apply to any enthusiasm displayed for guns or the military, proclivities of this sort being far too deeply imbedded in the American psyche. But an interest in Keats, Tennyson or Wordsworth is something that will now bear watching and worrying about.

If there is anything this country didn't need just now, it was for Tim McVeigh to serve as poetry's poster boy—any more than all those years ago it needed Norman Bates to exemplify a love for good music.

THE BLINDING DEMISE OF A SUPERSTAR

(Originally published in The Philadelphia Inquirer, July 2009)

Back on Dec. 6 of 2008, I e-mailed a little quiz to a number of friends, more than half of whom are my contemporaries—that is, over 60. Admonishing them not to cheat by using Google, I asked if they could name the "legendary songwriter, recording artist, guitarist, and Grammy winner whose premature death occurred 20 years ago today."

Although a few predictably guessed John Lennon—who was shot to death on Dec. 8, 1980—none got the right answer: Roy Orbison. But what really knocked me for a loop was the response from a former classmate, now an award-winning novelist, who, upon being told the correct answer, replied, "That figures. I love Roy Orbison but unfortunately didn't know he was dead."

It figures indeed. When the tragedy-plagued creator of such timeless tunes as "Blue Bayou," "Crying," "Oh, Pretty Woman," and "Only the Lonely" died of a massive heart attack at 52, he got a respectable amount of recognition, but nothing that couldn't have been easily missed.

If you did happen to catch his obituary in *The New York Times*, however, you would have read this comment from Bruce Springsteen: "His arrangements were complex and operatic. They had rhythm and movement, and they addressed the underside of pop romance. They were scary. His voice was unearthly."

A similar eulogy might have characterized the work of Dan Fogelberg, an incredibly gifted singer-songwriter who, over three decades, created some of the most exquisite melodies and poetic lyrics in the annals of pop music. Fogelberg's discography includes not only a number of double-platinum albums (and one triple-platinum), but, in my estimation, two of the finest collections ever produced by a recording artist:

REPEAT OFFENDERS

The Innocent Age (1981) and *Full Circle* (2003), which was the last to be released while he was alive.

Fogelberg died of prostate cancer at the age of 56 in December 2007, leaving many of his fans (myself included) with a profound sense of personal loss. Yet most newspapers carried just a modest wire story on his passing, and the evening news mentioned it only briefly.

The relatively reserved respects and trivial tributes the media accorded such prodigious talents become that much harder to swallow given the hype and histrionics that surrounded the recent death of Michael Jackson.

It wasn't just the wall-to-wall news coverage, of a sort ordinarily reserved for a president or pontiff. There were also the excessive exaltations emanating from various public figures, to the effect that Jackson was no less than the greatest genius ever known to the world of contemporary music.

A cultural icon, he may well have been, and there's no denying that his records outsold everyone else's. But to imply that Jackson's legacy to our musical culture outshined the contributions of all other artists, or that his talent was on a scale that somehow eclipsed theirs, is gratuitous and offensive to many of us (however out of the mainstream we might be) who may have found other music far more beguiling or aesthetically pleasing.

It's bad enough that some of our most gifted performers have gotten relatively little attention upon departing this mortal coil. But when the death of a superstar pulls in such an untoward amount of acclaim, it's almost as if some kind of massive artistic vacuum consumes all of our collective appreciation, leaving our society even more oblivious than usual to the brilliance of so many other stars in our firmament.

FILMDOM'S 'FINEST' IN FREE FALL

(Originally published in The SandPaper, September 2012)

Back during my journalistic 'basic training' as editor in chief of my college newspaper, I was approached by an eager-beaver type chap who wanted to write movie reviews. Since this would-be critic could show me nothing in the way of previous work, I asked him to provide us with a sample.

A couple days later, he was back with some ecstatic prose in praise of whatever film was currently playing at the local cinema, ending in the unforgettable line, "It is a very good movie that I soon hope to see."

What reminded me of that long-ago 'screening session' was reading about the latest choices of a group of 846 international critics for the "top ten films of all times," based on a poll taken once every decade and published in the British Film Institute's magazine. Or, more precisely, it was the realization that none of the works determined to be the cream of the cinematic crop had been released after 1968 (including three dating back to the silent-movie era).

I mean, how likely is it that even the most avid movie enthusiast has either found or will find an opportunity to watch Ozu's *Tokyo Story* (1953), Renior's *La Règle du jeu* (1939) or Murnau's *Sunrise: A Song for Two Humans* (1927), which were the third, fourth and fifth choices? Or, for that matter, their eight and ninth selections, the 1929 Soviet documentary *Man With a Movie Camera* and *The Passion of Joan of Arc* (1927)?

But what about the remaining films among the all-time top ten that contemporary viewers might either have seen or can still readily access? Well, let's start with the ones chosen to lead the latest list. It seems that after half a century of occupying the No. 1 spot, the controversial 1941 classic *Citizen Kane* has somehow been nudged into the No. 2 position by a "new" greatest film of all time—Alfred Hitchcock's 1958 psychological thriller *Vertigo*.

REPEAT OFFENDERS

Now whether or not you think the excessively melodramatic *Citizen Kane* actually merited its former top-of-the-heap designation, it would certainly qualify as having been perhaps the most provocative picture in Hollywood history—given newspaper baron William Randolph Hearst's attempts to not only censor it, but literally destroy it. But, then, one really can't blame Hearst, considering how its star, director and co-writer, the brash young novice Orson Welles, caricatured him in the movie and then killed him off a decade before his actual death (and Hearst was known to be especially averse to talk of his own demise). *Citizen Kane*, in fact, was about as precarious a proposition as any studio ever embarked on, and its very survival is something that makes it a singular achievements in the annals of filmdom.

Vertigo, however, is another story entirely—a mildly intriguing one at best with a plot device that even one of its more enthusiastic reviewers, *New York Times* critic Bosley Crowther, described as "devilishly far-fetched" and a character transformation that pushes the limits of credibility as well. It also features some of the most amateurish special effects graphics ever conceived in the pre-computer era. That as mediocre a mystery as *Vertigo* should have somehow managed to reach so dizzying a height of distinction is something that causes my head to spin.

But what I really would like to know is how such conventional cinematic fare is accorded an honor that I and many others believe rightfully belongs to a picture that has never been surpassed for historical grandeur, casting, acting, direction and all-around magnificence in more than 70 years. I'm referring, of course, to the 1939 production of Margaret Mitchell's *Gone with the Wind*. Despite the utter chaos that accompanied its filming—and the triteness of its opening description of the antebellum South—movie making just doesn't get any better than this, either then or now. Yet, incredibly enough, it is nowhere to be found on that roster of ten greatest films. Nor, for that matter, are two other vintage cinematic classics I would definitely regard as top-ten material—John Huston's *The African Queen* (1951) and Billy Wilder's Oscar-winning dramatic comedy, *The Apartment* (1960).

Probably somewhat more familiar to most contemporary viewers than the top two, however, is No. 6 on the critics' list—Stanley Kubrick's *2001: A Space Odyssey* from 1968. While it is, to be sure, a memorable and mesmerizing vision of what might happen were a computer to stage a mutiny during interplanetary travel, it is also, in retrospect, strictly a period piece whose time has quite literally come and gone—particularly now that cyberspace is where computer technology has taken us instead. And while John Ford's 1956 saga *The Searchers* (No. 7) may be one of the better westerns from those thrilling days of yesteryear that saw more than their share of cowboys and Indians, whether it truly deserves 'best-of-the-best' status is probably strictly in the eye of the beholder.

Then there's Italian filmmaker Federico Fellini's *8 ½*, currently in tenth place. This 1963 opus tells the story of a celebrated director's creative crisis—something Fellini actually suffered at the time—resulting in the 'unmaking' of the movie he is working on. It's interesting, but given all of its flashbacks and fantasies (as well as the fast-moving English subtitles), it can also be a bit confusing and difficult to follow in places. By contrast, a far more entertaining and explicit use of such cinematic navel-gazing can be found in the 2002 comedy *Adaptation*, which screenwriter Charlie Kaufman based on his own inability to turn the nonfiction book *The Orchid Thief* into a screenplay—a dilemma he ingenuously resolves with a somewhat bizarre twist at the end.

And that's just one example of the many fine films to have come along during the past four decades, many which could easily have been considered contenders for all-time top-ten status. To name just a few, there's *Patton* and *The Godfather* (both I and II) from the 1970s; *Ragtime, Amadeus, Driving Miss Daisy*, and *Glory*, the riveting depiction of the Civil War's first black regiment, all from the 1980s; the gripping (and very amusing) true-life legal drama *A Civil Action*, Martin Scorsese's nonfiction gangland epic *Goodfellas*, and the Coen Brothers' comic thriller *Fargo* from the 1990s, and Roman Polanski's *The Pianist* (2002) for best true-life saga of human survival.

But, oddly, none of these and other widely acknowledged screen masterpieces appear anywhere among the critics' supposed ten best films of all time, a list that consists largely of what appear to be some of the

REPEAT OFFENDERS

most antiquated and obscure opuses the participants could possibly come up with (and at that, without even giving a nod to the highly acclaimed 1930 anti-war epic, *All Quiet on the Western Front*).

It's almost as if these critics were making a point of advertising their arcane (as well as archaic) apprehension, not only by attempting to transform the transitory into the transcendent, but by canvassing cobweb-covered celluloid corners to find movies that most of us have never seen—and can never really hope to see.

WRITING WRONGS

THE AUTHORSHIP AUTHENTICITY GAP

(Originally published in The SandPaper, June 1996)

Before getting around to the subject of this particular essay, I would like to do something I have never before felt obliged to do in all the years I have been penning commentary. That is, I would like to assure everyone reading this dissertation that the actual person credited with writing it bears sole responsibility for its content.

My reason for doing so is to allay any doubts about its authorship that anyone (including my editor) might possibly be harboring after reading of an unseemly little episode that recently occurred here in New Jersey.

I'm referring to the appearance of two nearly identical opinion pieces in two separate newspapers—including the state's largest, the *Star-Ledger* of Newark—under different bylines, both of which belonged to local officials in different parts of the state.

A one-in-a-trillion coincidence, perhaps? Afraid not. The similarity of the two op-eds, as it turned out, was due to their having been one and the same article, written by an individual whose identity, unfortunately, matched that of neither of the two purported "authors."

The real author, as you may have guessed by now, was actually a scribe for a public relations firm—in this case, one representing Donald Trump's casino enterprises and other gaming establishments in their efforts to block funding of a proposed $300 million Atlantic City road-tunnel project that would benefit a potential competitor.

To the PR operation, it was little more than business as usual, with a spokesman defending such ghostwriting practices as common on editorial pages. But the newspapers involved were plainly put out. "We expect contributions...to be original work, not regurgitated lobbying from some public relations firm," was the reaction from *Star-Ledger* editor James Wilse. That concept, he added, seemed to be eluding the politician who had claimed authorship and his press aide, who had served as the middleman.

It's only natural, of course that it would—just as the practice of producing prose by proxy in the world of big business and politics (what many consider to be the "Real World") might tend to elude the relatively innocent, if supposedly cynical souls who inhabit the comparatively cloistered world of the newsroom.

And given the fact that newspaper opinion pages frequently provide a meeting place for these antithetical worlds, a collision of sorts was probably bound to occur sooner or later over the issue of the authorship authenticity gap.

To fully understand how such a gap evolved in our society, it might be a good idea to go back and review the undergraduate careers of those on either side of it—particularly the college courses that required the writing of term papers.

For some, such assignments meant spending many hours in the library diligently taking notes on little index cards for eventual use in honest attempts at original composition—a process that also provided training at working night after night into the wee hours.

Many others, however, found it far less of a hassle to simply buy a slick, professionally prepared term paper from one of the various companies or individuals who routinely sold them (an absolute necessity for those whose education was deficient in basic writing skills). Having thus paid for relief from an onerous burden, they were then free to spend their time in endless, noisy fraternizing, often to the consternation of their more conscientious classmates.

Far from failing such slackers, however, college was actually doing for them exactly what it was designed to do—that is, preparing them to enter the Real World of big business and politics.

The world of big business, they soon discovered, was not all that different from their college experience in one key respect: its standard operating procedure was simply to pay someone else to do whatever writing one's job supposedly required. The relatively simple tasks could always be relegated to a literate secretary, while the more important and creative ones (such as the annual letter to stockholders that appeared over the signature of the CEO) were entrusted to an advertising or PR agency (which, after being hired by the company's creative department, might in turn engage a freelancer to do the actual work). The result was, again, greater freedom to fraternize, only this time either in endless meetings or on the golf course.

For those who entered politics, the pattern became even more pronounced, with whole cadres of writers often enlisted to pen the speeches, promises, attacks on opponents and other hype that would ultimately be attributed to the candidate or office holder (and which is one reason why politicians so frequently seem to forget the positions they took in preceding years).

All this, naturally, required having to recruit genuine writers from the ranks of those former students who had taken the trouble to complete their own term papers—the ones, that is, who were shrewd enough to ascertain what was going on in the Real World and get in on the high-stakes action by allowing others to take credit for their words. (Some even discovered more unique applications, such as ghosting celebrity "autobiographies" or answering fan mail to soap-opera stars.)

There were those, however, who remained conscientious to the core, stubbornly persisting in being solely responsible for their written efforts. It was this group that ended up providing the labor pool for the nation's newsrooms—coming to regard as a normal state of affairs the task of having to churn out vast volumes of prose on a daily basis (and often into the wee hours) more often than not for relatively modest recompense.

Not that their job doesn't offer other types of gratification—for instance, the pleasure of occasionally forcing someone from the world of big business or politics to eat their own words. To expect them to actually write their own words, though, may be asking entirely too much.

Author's note: Since this article appeared, those little index cards once used in writing term papers have been replaced by such online shortcuts as Google and its clones. This has no doubt encouraged a certain amount of plagiarism—which may account for the increased instances of newspaper reporters and columnists being fired for turning in unoriginal work.

A PRIZE PIECE OF PREVARICATION

(Originally published in The SandPaper, January 1997)

Recently, some correspondence was delivered to our mailbox whose contents I found more than a bit unsettling, considering the source and apparent intent. Emblazoned with the logo of Publishers Clearing House, it conveyed an invitation to conspire with that supposedly reputable organization in a scheme to deliberately deceive the media, and hence the American public as well.

Arriving in an envelope bearing the word "WINNER" in large red letters, the missive in question came addressed to my sister bearing the signature of one David Sayer, identified as "Executive Director, Prize Patrol." It opens by urging her to get used to hearing that term—"winner"—because that's what folks will be calling her should Mr. Sayer show up at our house on Super Bowl Sunday to announce on live TV that she has won $10 million.

Mr. Sayer then goes on to reveal what he's already done in "happy anticipation" of that announcement—namely, "taken the liberty" of drafting an attached press release that "will be issued to hundreds of newspapers, and to radio and television stations from coast to coast." All she need do is assent to its use—"paying particular attention to the bolded paragraph"—to receive an additional payment of $5,000."

The spurious (and presumptuous) nature of the release involved, however, became evident from sentence one, which describes how "the excitement of Super Bowl Sunday was intensified for the Bonvies" by the appearance of the Publishers Clearing House Prize Patrol with its "life-changing news."

Now, it may be true that the Bonvie household hasn't yet reached the point of becoming so blasé as to be rendered incapable of excitement should the Publishers Clearing House Prize Patrol actually show up at its front door. But if there is one thing that unfailingly fails to generate even so much as a jolt of excitement within its confines, it is the institution known as "Super Bowl Sunday."

As shocking and seemingly un-American as such an admission may be to popular sensibilities, the fact is that our "household" is apparently incapable of being carried away (or even mildly moved) by the spectacle of two teams in which we have no financial stake, usually representing cities in which we neither reside nor have any roots, competing in a third such metropolis for top honors in a sport that, frankly, holds little interest for us (unlike, say, baseball).

In fact, I suspect that untold numbers of otherwise solid citizens secretly share those sentiments, but fear coming out of the closet, lest they be besieged by a mob bearing torches along with "Super Bowl: love it or leave" placards and demanding their immediate deportation back to wherever it is was their ancestors came here from.

But let's get back to Mr. Sayer's advance press release, which becomes even more prone to prevarication as it proceeds to attribute to my sister the words, "I can't believe it...It's the dream of a lifetime come true," with absolutely no guarantee or promise that she would say any such thing if actually confronted by the Prize Patrol. In fact, I think it just as likely she would simply say "Wow!" or be rendered temporarily speechless, especially when suddenly finding herself the subject of a live telecast to "millions of Americans from coast to coast."

It was that all-important bolded paragraph, however, that really startled me—the "ten million dollar question" of whether my sister had ordered any magazines as well as entering the sweepstakes. It boldly proclaimed that "Sayer was pleased to report that, yes," she "is a good customer," recently having placed an unspecified order (for which a blank space is designated). And while adding that no purchase is actually necessary to win, he says he is also "clearly delighted that a friend of the Clearing House took away the big prize."

At this point, the raising of another question seems in order—whether or not Mr. Sayer fully understands the implications of what he's saying.

Let's suppose, for argument's sake, that one goes along with the somewhat dubious premise that the act of ordering periodicals automatically makes one not merely a customer, but an actual "friend." Isn't there something just a wee bit suspect about a sweepstakes in which the top prize just happens to be awarded to a "friend" of the sponsor?

Now ordinarily, I'd be the last person to presume to tell my sister what to do. But in this case, I feel compelled to strongly advise her against the subscription to *Consumer Reports* she was contemplating placing with Publisher's Clearing House. That's because, should she actually succeed in having that Prize Patrol show up outside the door, the last thing we'd want would be to in any way jeopardize her right to that top award through even an appearance of impropriety.

And while I'm at it, I'll probably try to talk her out of approving the use of that advance press release as well. While the prospect of an extra five grand might seem very tempting to her right now, one she's pocketed the ten mil, it'll hardly seem worth lying to all those media outlets just for the purpose of picking up some extra pocket change.

Author's note: In the years since this was written, my sister, encouraged by friends, has become somewhat more tuned into football, while baseball remains the only spectator sport that holds my interest. I do, however, attempt to feign enthusiasm for the Super Bowl (so as not to appear a bad sport), and, as a former copywriter, actually find the commercials somewhat intriguing. As for Publishers Clearing House, it is still going strong, only now has expanded into all manner of merchandise. David Sayer not only remains affiliated with the Prize Patrol he founded, but is now on Facebook, where he offers "a clip of some priceless winning moments" and notes that "PCH employees do not send friend requests or private messages on Facebook" and "NEVER notify winners on Facebook or by phone." He also urges us to "Watch out for scammers."

ABBREVIATION ABUSE: A 'CAPITAL' OFFENSE

(Originally published in The SandPaper, October 2002)

With all the attention now being devoted to various, and quite serious, forms of abuse, such as child abuse, spousal abuse, human-rights abuse, substance abuse (which is actually a contorted term for self-abuse) and abuse of the public trust, it would probably ill-behoove me to introduce yet another abuse classification to our manifest of malfeasance. Especially when the abuse at issue is the sort of thing that many people might consider too petty to even be worth mentioning, let along making an issue of.

Nevertheless, having spent a considerable part of my checkered career employed as a copy editor for various newspapers, and thus being more apt to notice things of this sort than my less picky compatriots, I'm afraid that I can remain silent on this subject no longer.

Abbreviation abuse, my friends, has become rampant in our culture.

That's right, abbreviation abuse—meaning the unauthorized and improper application of designations intended for postal use only, and in particular the reprehensible practice of substituting them for legitimate state abbreviations.

While you may well think this to be a matter of the utmost triviality, its impact on the quality of our written communications has been a most unfortunate one indeed.

It isn't just that these bureaucratic IDs represent a radical departure from what the founding fathers of the language intended to be the standard and accepted forms of abridgement (as duly recorded in the Associated Press Stylebook, which to the best of my knowledge is still considered the definitive guide in such matters), and hence a creeping form of government intrusion on our traditional terminology. It's also the manner in which these clumsy and inappropriate upper-case interruptions in sentence flow have managed to accelerate the erosion of our society's ability to express itself.

REPEAT OFFENDERS

To my somewhat purist sensibilities, in fact, such disorderly linguistic conduct is nothing short of a capital offense.

While examples of it are everywhere, the ones that bother me the most are those commonly found on the obituary pages of some newspapers, where unedited tributes for which the relatives of the deceased are charged have replaced traditional staff-written obits. Perhaps it's because I have worked at various times as an obituary-page editor who went to considerable pains to see that both accuracy and stylistic standards were maintained, but I wince whenever I read such awkward alphabet-soup sentences as: "Mr. Jones was born in Mason City, IA, raised in Ogden, UT, moved here 30 years ago from Lowell, MA and retired last year to Scottsdale, AZ."

Perhaps even worse is the detrimental effect this appears to be having on the sanctity of long-established principles of punctuation. As a direct result, we are now living through a period in which the use of periods to identify abbreviations has all but disappeared. Thus not only do we find repeated references to NJ—which should read N.J. except when used with a ZIP code—but to US (as in US citizens), sans the periods that once signified that those letters actually stood for something (other than just "us," that is).

And now that we've declared open season on one class of period, could the end be in sight as well for those we use to end sentences? Might our written pages one day read like so much free-association blather, with no thought given to designating where one thought concludes and another begins?

It was bad enough when such an ill-informed practice was merely indulged in by misguided members of the public. Now, however, it has gone well beyond the individual stage and become institutionalized by media, as I discovered not too long ago when I chanced to tune in the ubiquitous Cable News Network and read some of the updates that appear in the form of streams of text at the bottom of the screen.

First, there was the "AL mom" arrested for putting her child in the oven. Then came the item about Prof. Quincy Troupe being chosen "CA's first poet laureate." CNN, it was evident, had quite literally "gone postal," setting an egregious example for its millions of viewers who have no reason to doubt its knowledge of what constitutes not only legitimate news, but appropriate abbreviation policy.

Now ordinarily, I consider myself to be a rather tolerant person—suffering grammatical foolishness patiently, if not exactly gladly. I've stood by speechlessly, for example, at the sight of possessive apostrophes inserted in purely plural nouns by various retail establishments (e.g., free refill's) or on the cute little name emblems that some couples like to post outside their doors (e.g., The Gaffney's). I've even refrained from telling the owners of costly neon signs that they lacked hyphens in crucial places, or, worse yet, contained them where they quite obviously didn't belong (e.g., "Appliances-for-less"), even while recoiling from the sight.

But when abbreviations are abused in this manner, I feel compelled to speak out—and to attempt to do whatever I can to correct the situation. To that end, I offer a rule that I hope you'll keep in mind: If it has two capital letters and no periods, and you're not using it in conjunction with an official ZIP code, it's not OK. Nor, for that matter, is it OK to use OK as the abbreviation for Oklahoma, which is still Okla.—unless, again, it's placed alongside a Zip code listing for some locale within that state (OK also being the form of the word denoting approval or agreement that's officially sanctioned by the AP stylebook, which notes "Do not use okay"—although the dictionary seems to prefer an O.K. version).

Oh, and one other thing: when in doubt, spell it out.

Author's note: We now seem to have reached the point where the substitution of zip code designations for state abbreviations and the use of abbreviations without periods has become so rampant as to corrupt the language itself and render corrections all but futile. And the trendiness of Twitter, with its limit on characters, has definitely not been helpful.

OBSERVATION PLATFORMS

'SLIP SLIDING AWAY' TOWARD OBLIVION

(Originally published in The SandPaper, March 2001)

Increasingly these days I have an uncanny feeling of having been transported to an alien planet, one not unlike the otherworldly imitation of earth depicted by Ray Bradbury in *The Martian Chronicles*.

It's the kind of planet that looks and seems pretty much like the one I've grown to know and love—that is, until I chance to bring up some celebrated personage, only to have one or more of the other inhabitants say, "Who's that?"

Now, it's one thing not to know who Ray Bradbury is, since sci-fi writers, even the more celebrated ones, tend to be known to only a certain percentage of the population. But how about performers of supposed worldwide renown—for example, Paul Simon? Surely, there couldn't be a person alive (or at least living in the Western Hemisphere) who isn't aware of the man and his contributions to popular culture.

Or so I thought—until, on a recent visit to my neighborhood supermarket, I happened to find myself engaged in a casual checkout line discussion of the Great Bogus Blizzard of '01 (the monster storm that never quite materialized in these parts, despite the dire warnings of weather forecasters).

Observing how this much heralded non-event had managed to confound the most sophisticated technology devised by humans, I noted that it seemed to illustrate the Paul Simon lyrics: "God only knows/ God makes his plan/ The information's unavailable to the mortal man." To which the clerk, a lass of 17, responded that not only was she unfamiliar with the song, "Slip Sliding Away," she'd never even heard of the singer/songwriter (whom I had just assumed was still popular after all these years).

In an attempt to validate the vision long planted in my brain of certain individuals having achieved permanent stardom, I ventured, "But, surely, you've heard of Simon and Garfunkel?"

"Afraid not," came the reply.

Now admittedly, this wasn't the first time I'd been hit with the realization of just how far removed today's teens and twenty-somethings have strayed from the familiar world occupied by my generation. It's a phenomenon, in fact, that came to my attention a few years ago, when, as a copy editor for a fairly sizable daily newspaper, I was often charged with putting together the "People" column, which meant having to select and write headlines and captions for celebrity-related news items.

Much to my astonishment, I soon discovered that the young women charged with pagination responsibilities, all of whom were recently out of school, were totally unacquainted with some of the biggest names of the era in which I grew up. After the initial shock wore off, I chalked it up to that proverbial "generation gap" which I had apparently crossed at some point without ever quite realizing it.

Since then, however, I have been discovering that this chasm is quite a bit deeper and more extensive than anyone in my age group might ever have guessed.

As it turned out, it isn't just such older show-biz legends as Bing Crosby, Jimmy Durante, Billie Holiday, Rosemary Clooney or the Mills Brothers who stir not the slightest hint of recognition in youthful circles. It's also the performers that helped establish my generation's cultural identity—transcendent talents on the order of Neil Diamond, Linda Ronstadt and Gordon Lightfoot—who appear to have been not only pushed off the contemporary Walk of Fame, but even evicted from Memory Lane by an influx of transitory, largely uninspired counterfeit celebrities who might as well have arrived from Mars.

The phenomenon of top stars of the recent past drawing blank stares, however, is only the most obvious symptom of a far more serious form of cultural amnesia afflicting today's emerging adult population.

It's positively bewildering, for instance, to discover how few of the members of this group have any familiarity whatsoever with the Warren Commission. Or Watergate. Or, for that matter, *Gone with the Wind*, despite the numerous times the film's been aired on TV. They may know a lot about computer technology, but talk with them for a brief time and you're soon apt to discover that they really don't know much about history—or, for that matter, anything at all that occurred before they entered grade school (with the possible exception of The Beatles, who may yet prove to be one of our last surviving links to yesterday).

This break with the past, especially the recent past, is perhaps comparable to global warming in the threat it poses to our collective sense of continuity. For the more we fail to imbue the up-and-coming generation with an understanding of just who and what helped bring us to the place we currently occupy in time and space, the more our familiar world will start to resemble an alien planet.

And the more we'll be slip sliding away toward oblivion.

Author's note: In the decade since this essay first appeared, the cultural amnesia to which it refers seems to have significantly worsened, just as the parade of counterfeit celebrities has continued unabated (aided and abetted by the glorification of amateur talent on prime-time television) and popular music has all but ceased to be anything resembling music as we once knew it.

A PITCH FOR 'HOME TEAMS' TO LIVE UP TO THEIR BILLING

(Originally published in The SandPaper, July 2002)

While not exactly what you might call a spectator-sports enthusiast, I've always been partial to baseball. Partial, that is, to the extent that I've been known to waste the better part of an evening watching the game on the tube, usually if the Red Sox were playing, and especially if they were playing the Yankees.

I seldom have been known to venture out to ballparks, however (not having been to one, in fact, since I was 12, when I accompanied a friend and his dad to Yankee Stadium). Perhaps that has something to do with the lyrics from that famous song, "Take Me Out to the Ball Game"—the part about "I don't care if we never get back." I, for one, do care very much if I get back (and the current movie, *The Sum of All Fears*, in which a stadium full of people gets vaporized by terrorists, hasn't helped in this regard).

In spite of any such trepidation, though, and the fact that even after years of residing in South Jersey, I've never really become very much of a Phillies fan (as treasonous-sounding an admission as that might be), I did chance to visit Veterans Stadium recently at the invitation of someone who had won a set of tickets on a radio station promotion.

But while I can't say the experience wasn't fun, there were also some things about it that struck this stranger to the 'stadiumscape' as just a little bit strange.

I mean, here I was at the scene of the action that always sounds so exciting when you tune it in on the small screen. And yet, despite a series of rousing plays, a seesaw match between the Phillies and Baltimore Orioles, a couple of injuries and an apparently heated argument over a controversial call, the game I was witnessing seemed strangely devoid of drama.

REPEAT OFFENDERS

But perhaps that's because all of this was merely seen and not heard. Aside from the crack of the bat, the odd announcement of a batter's name or a pitching change, and some occasional musical accompaniment, there was no communication of what was transpiring down there on the field, or, indeed, that a new inning was even in progress.

Thus, although sitting directly above first base, I managed to miss two separate leadoff doubles, once while momentarily distracted by the antics of the Phillies Phanatic (which somehow seemed more entertaining than the game itself). Not only did the muted effect make it difficult to follow the action, but it also seemed to me to create a distinct sense of detachment between the players and those who came to see them play.

To compensate somewhat for this feeling of being somehow disconnected from the game, I eventually began reciting my own running account of the action, much to the apparent amusement of some fans sitting in front of us. Such was their response, in fact, that I momentarily began to wonder whether I shouldn't have tried sportscasting for a living.

Several days later, I placed a call to the Phillies' front office, and asked one of the team's PR people whether not having an announcer provide play-by-play commentary was currently standard procedure. It was at all the big-league ballparks he'd recently been to, he replied—although exactly when and why it had become so, he couldn't say. He thought it might have something to do with broadcast rights.

Not that this seemed to diminish the enthusiasm of the fans at the stadium, some of them barely out of diapers, whose obvious devotion to the team was reflected in either spirited, rousing cheers and applause or loud outbursts of booing. While such ardor, I realized, is a traditional and intrinsic part of the sport, it too, gave me pause.

So while I had that PR guy on the phone, I asked a question that those displays of passion had brought to mind: Could he tell me just how many of the 25 active players on the Phillies roster that night actually came from the Philadelphia area?

"There are a few people," he replied. But when pressed to be more specific, he could think of only one —Doug Glanville, who hailed from

Hackensack, N.J. (a New York City suburb) and had attended the University of Pennsylvania.

But then he added, "There's so much scouting and players being recruited from all over the world, teams just can't afford to look at the surrounding area."

Which got me to wondering: Why can't they? Granted, Major League Baseball (along with other professional spectator sports) is a highly competitive form of big business, and owners want the benefit of the best talent available. But shouldn't at least some of that talent – say, a certain quota—be truly a reflection of the individual locale each team purports to represent? Given all the recent revisions regarding the competitive structure of the game, can't it also be ordained that when we " root, root, root for the home team," what we're rooting for is at least to some degree a hometown institution?

Or perhaps you think it highly meddlesome for someone who hadn't been to an actual ball game in years to suddenly start pitching proposals for major-league change in our national pastime.

But, hey, I calls' em as I sees 'em.

Author's note: On a whim, I mailed the original published version of this essay to the curmudgeonly 60 Minutes commentator Andy Rooney, who was a baseball buff. A couple months later, I received a reply—a note typed the old-fashioned way (complete with corrections) that said, "Dear Bill, I seem to be a little behind on my mail, but I got your letter and the baseball column, which I enjoyed reading. Regards, Andrew A. Rooney," along with his signature. Which was somewhat extraordinary in light of what he told an interviewer shortly before his death in 2011—that he seldom answered the multitude of letters he received, and never gave autographs because "what kind of idiot wants my name on a piece of paper?"

SPACE TRAVEL JUST ISN'T WHAT IT USED TO BE

(Originally published in The Record of Bergen County and The Philadelphia Inquirer, August 2005)

It was a cinematic coincidence that ranks up there with the debut of *The China Syndrome* just a few days before the 1979 nuclear accident at Three Mile Island. I'm referring to the news of the discovery of a 10th planet in our solar system on the same day a network showed the movie *K-Pax*, in which a mental patient who claims to be from another world tells his psychologist that 10 planets, in fact, revolve around the sun.

Apart from the bizarre timing, the observation by Kevin Spacey's self-proclaimed spaceman was one of the rare occasions when conjecture of this sort has turned out to be the right stuff. (Assuming that astronomers don't now go and further alter the equation by, say, downsizing Pluto to the status of a mere planetoid, as some have suggested.)

In fact, few things in life have proved as disappointing to me as the gradual descent of the elevated expectations with which I was imbued during my 1950s childhood by repeated exposure to sci-fi writers' predilection for misguided predictions.

In retrospect, I suppose I should have been rendered more skeptical of such speculation by something I read at the impressionable age of 9 in a serious-minded, down-to-earth science booklet called "Our Ocean of Air" (one of a number of such publications I received as a weekly reward for good behavior at a private school I attended). I can even recall the wording: "No one has ever gone beyond our ocean of air. Probably, no one ever will go."

Despite its seemingly authoritative imprimatur, however, it left me thoroughly (and, it turned out, correctly) unconvinced that the sky was the limit of our exploration. What I was far more inclined to believe was that we'd be quite well-entrenched in outer space by the time I reached my 30s, as indicated by the authors of a number of sci-fi books published by the John C. Winston Co. (which were to me every bit as fascinating as the *Harry Potter* tales are to kids of the same age today).

Despite my having already moved on by then to far more sophisticated reading material (including having read all 1,000-plus pages of *Gone With the Wind* at the age of 10), these volumes, with their preadolescent heroes, were what regularly drew me to the children's library just a few doors from my elementary school in Milford, Conn.

Readily identifiable by their spaceship logo, the ones that dealt with space exploration—in contrast to the more fanciful and less-credible realm of time travel—bore such intriguing titles as *Marooned on Mars*, *Five Against Venus*, and my favorite, *Vandals of the Void* by Jack Vance, a saga of space pirates who plunder interplanetary passenger shuttles. In addition to giving me an appreciation of alliteration, the book enthralled me with its descriptions of such characters as Crazy Sam Baxter, the moon-ruby prospector who ends up at the bottom of Baxter's bottomless pit, and Professor Dexter, the mild-mannered academician who ultimately reveals himself to be The Basilisk, a fiendish 'supervillain' who could well have served as the inspiration for Darth Vader. (All of which, I might add, was supposed to have taken place well before the end of the last century.)

Nor did the anticipation that everyday transit between planets was just over the horizon diminish with the advent of manned space flight, as evidenced by the movie *2001: A Space Odyssey*, released in 1968. That was the year before American astronauts first set foot on the moon (an event that my elderly aunt characterized as being "fine for younger people"). It was a year when it looked as though we were well on the way to fulfilling all those sci-fi prophecies. The movie, however, missed the mark by envisioning a maniacal mainframe computer running amok in deep space while failing to foresee the menace arising from personal computers being sabotaged in cyberspace.

Since then, aside from a few unmanned probes such as the one sent off this month to collect data about Mars, it's almost as though we've gotten stalled somewhere just beyond our ocean of air, our efforts mainly confined to the launching of utilitarian satellites; the tedious, long-term construction of an orbiting space station; and the occasional shuttle flight undertaken to service the space station amid rising trepidation about safety. (True, a company called Space Adventures has just announced plans to offer rides around the far side of the moon for $100 million per trip. But that's a far cry from the routine rocket traffic envisioned by starry-eyed 20th-century forecasters.)

Perhaps such stagnation of our once stellar ambitions is due to our collaboration with the Russians, who spurred us on to new heights back in the days when we considered them rivals. Whatever the reason, at the rate we've been advancing in space travel, there seems little likelihood that we'll be sending out any manned expeditions to that 10th planet within the foreseeable future—let alone have the opportunity to visit it ourselves.

Author's note: The year after this essay first appeared, Pluto was downgraded to the status of a "dwarf planet," as was the supposed 10th planet discovered in 2005, with the result that our solar system now consists of eight full-fledged planets and five dwarf planets, according to Fraser Cain, publisher of Universe Today. And we still haven't returned to the moon—although in July 2013, the House Science Committee approved a NASA authorization bill rejecting a proposed manned mission to an asteroid in favor of revisiting the lunar landscape, perhaps as soon as 2020, and maybe even proceeding on to Mars.

RAINING ON OUR CHARADE

(Originally published in The Philadelphia Inquirer, May 2001)

Is it my imagination, or does Memorial Day seem to attract more than its share of dampness and downpour? If this year's observance should also be rained on, I, for one, will welcome the dismal and overcast skies, which I consider even more suited to the occasion than snow on Christmas.

The Veterans of Foreign Wars would like to see the official observance of Memorial Day fixed on May 30, rather than used as the anchor of a three-day weekend, and I find myself agreeing. The occasion, the VFW believes, should be one of high seriousness, which hardly characterizes the way Memorial Day is now observed.

Today, what Memorial Day rather represents for most Americans is a celebration of summer's arrival. That does a disservice to those we're supposed to be remembering.

While I'm neither particularly religious nor a flag-waving patriot, I find the arrival of a soggy Memorial Day weekend to be a case for the existence of divine intervention. In fact, I believe that every time it rains on Memorial Day, it's really God raining on our charade.

For despite the laments of TV newscasters about the weather throwing a damper on our "official-start-of-summer" fun, this particular holiday was not one designed for picnics in the park, romps in the surf, or similar light-hearted activities. It was, rather, set aside to remember the multitudes of Americans in uniform whose lives were cut short by the wars this country has fought (whether justified or not is immaterial). The original idea is that Americans would decorate the graves of those who have served—as well as aiding and assisting those they left behind.

In other words, it was meant to be a sober, somber, and solemn occasion.

REPEAT OFFENDERS

But that concept became sadly corrupted during the late 1960s when Congress in its wisdom decided to move the observance from May 30 to the last Monday of the month so that Americans could enjoy (and businesses could profit from) a three-day holiday weekend. Thus evolved the somewhat perverse notion that on Memorial Day, we're all entitled to kick off our shoes, relax and let the good times roll — that is, if only the weather would cooperate.

That's why I think the VFW is right on target in calling for the traditional observance of Memorial Day to be moved back to May 30. Such a move would help restore the holiday's true intent and keep it from being hijacked for recreational purposes. In the meantime, it wouldn't hurt to pause for the National Moment of Remembrance at 3 p.m. that was declared by the White House last year, if for no other reason than to reflect on the lessons of history that could help prevent future generations from losing so much of their potential to unnecessary and avoidable conflicts.

Not that there's anything wrong with using the start of the summer season per se as an excuse for a three-day holiday weekend (or using the weekend as an excuse to shift into summer mode). Perhaps the sun itself would be more inclined to shine on such an occasion — as opposed to Memorial Day, when it seems far more fitting that the heavens open up and weep.

Author's note: Since this article was published, more than 6,600 members of the U.S. military died in "unnecessary and avoidable conflicts" — not to mention more than 50,000 who have been wounded, and the many, many thousands more diagnosed with post-traumatic stress disorder or traumatic brain injuries. And Memorial Day is still the excuse for a three-day holiday weekend.

THE CONSTITUTION, NOT THE FLAG, IS WHAT NEEDS PROTECTING

(Originally published in The Philadelphia Inquirer, July 2006)

Lately, there has been an awful lot of talk about making certain practices that some Americans find offensive unconstitutional. Since such demand seems to emanate chiefly from people who tend to engage in more than the average share of prayer, it raises the question of whether there might be a connection.

Perhaps these folks are simply under the misunderstanding that prayers all end with the word "amend."

Whatever the basis of their thinking, such *amendniks* seem to view the Constitution not so much as a guarantee of liberty and justice for all, than as one of unquestioning loyalty and mandated morality for all.

What they may have forgotten is what happened the last time a crusade rooted in virtue and "values" and driven by that old-time religion managed to capture the Holy Grail of a constitutional amendment. The upshot was that the sale of intoxicating beverages was outlawed, meaning that only outlaws had the ability to supply the public with intoxicating beverages. As a result, the Constitution ended up having to be re-amended.

Then again, perhaps the attempts of the latter-day Carrie Nations to impose new restraints on marginal rather than mainstream activities do reflect some degree of awareness that there is only so far a society such as ours can be taken on a forced march down the paths of righteousness.

While the battle of the bottle may have ultimately been lost due to popular resistance, the assumption seems to be that the public will be far less likely to protest prohibitions directed against same-sex marriage or flag desecration. But unlike the ill-fated 18th Amendment, which did succeed for a time in profoundly altering the mores, if not the morals, of American society, such proposed changes in the Constitution would likely have no effect whatsoever on our culture or conduct.

Non-heterosexual couples would continue living together as before—that is, without formal recognition of their status or recourse to certain legal and economic benefits—and folks who dislike America or its policies would go right on occasionally torching or otherwise desecrating the flag (just as used-car salesmen would go on using it as a prop to help promote the sale of their clunkers).

What would be altered, however, is the importance of the Constitution itself, which would have been profoundly degraded by being used not as the blueprint for a democratic society, but as a handy hook upon which affronted citizens and opportunistic politicians can hang blue laws and red herrings anytime they desire.

I therefore would like to propose a constitutional amendment of my own, one aimed at preserving the sanctity and integrity of the one thing that actually defines the freedoms symbolized by the American flag, which are what so many of our countrymen have actually fought and died for.

I'm talking about a prohibition on frivolously proposed constitutional amendments, a prohibition that would invest the idea voiced by President Bush that "an amendment to the Constitution is never to be undertaken lightly."

But what, you might ask, constitutes a frivolous constitutional amendment?

I'll let those sufficiently skilled translate this into politico-legalese, but I would say a frivolous amendment would be any proposed measure to render unconstitutional something that might offend some people but would do nothing whatsoever to help promote our collective rights to life, liberty and the pursuit of happiness.

If that doesn't give you a clear idea of what I mean, just think about what the late Supreme Court Justice Potter Stewart said in attempting to categorize pornography: "I know it when I see it."

IN DEFENSE OF OUR GOD-GIVEN RIGHT TO 'SUE THE BASTARDS'

(Originally published in The SandPaper, May 2008)

One of the most intriguing revelations I ever remember having come upon was that contained in a book I read some years ago titled *The Devil in Massachusetts: A Modern Inquiry into the Salem Witch Trials* by the late New England historian Marion L. Starkey.

After chronicling the hysteria that gripped the village of Salem when a group of young girls took to accusing various individuals of the crime of witchcraft, for which a number of them were subsequently convicted and hanged, the author provided this anecdotal note about what proved to be the antidote:

"Finally, the girls met their match. They cried out on a gentleman in Boston and the latter took novel action; he sent a 'writ to arrest these accusers in one thousand pound action of defamation' and entrusted local friends to put the accusers under observation. So coldly legal an act had a chastening effect; adolescents tough enough to watch a hanging without a qualm blanched at the idea of someone's having to pay a thousand pounds; their voices became discreet and then fell silent altogether."

What brought that particular passage to mind was Sen. John McCain's stated reason for opposing a Senate bill that would have made it easier for women to sue their employers for paying them less than male coworkers. The bill, which was narrowly defeated, came in response to a particularly mean-spirited Supreme Court decision that overturned a large jury award give to a woman named Lilly Ledbetter who had clearly been a victim of pay discrimination during the two decades she spent working as a supervisor at a Goodyear plant.

It wasn't that the Arizona senator was against "pay equity for women" per se. It was just that, as he explained it, "this kind of legislation...opens us up to lawsuits for all kinds of problems."

Would McCain, I couldn't help wondering, have harbored similar sentiments had he been living in Massachusetts back around 1691? Assuming he wouldn't have been in favor of witch hunting, do you suppose he would have been against giving its victims recourse to an effective legal counter-offensive?

The notion that we're burdened by too many lawsuits, especially those of a "frivolous" nature, is one that conservatives have tried for many years to push down our collective throats. The picture they paint is one of enterprise extinguished, companies crippled, institutions intimidated, doctors driven out of business and courts clogged by a veritable tidal wave of largely unnecessary and capricious litigation, advanced, aided and abetted by an army of avaricious attorneys.

They've even gone so far as to attempt to curtail the right to sue, an example being the Bush Administration's ongoing effort to "preempt" suits against pharmaceutical companies if the damages sought are in regard to a product that has been given the U.S. Food and Drug Administration's seal of approval.

Typifying this anti-litigation propaganda campaign is the Web site of the "Institute for Legal Reform," an affiliate of the U.S. Chamber of Commerce. It features a flash presentation under the headline, "I Am Lawsuit Abuse," which invites visitors to hear the stories told by various people who feel they were unfairly targeted by legal proceedings, such as the couple whose dry-cleaning establishment was sued for $67 million by an administrative law judge for having supposedly lost a pair of pants.

There's no denying that claims for damages may occasionally appear ridiculous or get out of hand. But such extreme examples of exploitation of the legal system are no justification for denying untold numbers of individuals who have been victimized by carelessness, negligence, greed, stupidity, discrimination or malicious behavior their right to seek compensation, relief or just plain justice.

That right, in fact, is one of our fundamental freedoms, grounded in the Seventh Amendment to the U.S. Constitution, which states, "in suits at common law...the right of trial by jury shall be preserved." While its application may be replete with complexities and interpretations, those who attempt to put restrictions on it are engaged in nothing short of an assault on one of the very foundation stones of the republic.

If anything, the ability of citizens to resort to civil action is probably underused, due to both the cost of legal help when a case can't be taken on contingency and general ignorance of the prerogatives they have under the law (such as the right to sue debt collectors for engaging in harassing tactics or violations of the Fair Debt Collection Practices Act).

In addition to the recourse it provides individuals, the right to seek legal redress for injury, insult, or inequity has historically been a major driving force in bringing about legal and social progress. Just as litigation was responsible for curtailing the witch hunts of 1691, for instance, it also was a key factor in ending institutionalized segregation in 1954 when the Supreme Court rendered its landmark ruling in Brown vs. Board of Education. It also can act as a powerful deterrent to the kinds of slipshod practices and shoddy products that often cause injury or death (yes, fewer people are probably scalded by hot coffee today as a result of that much-maligned judgment rendered by a jury against McDonald's some years back).

Especially important in this regard has been the process of discovery invoked by civil actions, which has brought to light many revelations impacting public health and safety that corporations and institutions would have much preferred remained secret.

The propensity of lawsuits to generate genuine reform, no doubt, is a large part of the reason they are anathema to so-called "reformers" whose actual interests lie in perpetuating the status quo.

Not that their efforts to chip away at the right that is so important in protecting all the others we've inherited haven't already met with some success. By giving President Bush eight years to reshape the Supreme Court in an even more conservative mold than it was when he took office, we've practically guaranteed that deserving plaintiffs, such as Lily Ledbetter, will have their attempts to obtain justice arbitrarily quashed.

REPEAT OFFENDERS

And you can just bet that if McCain were to be given the same opportunity, even fewer cases that reach the high court would end up being equitably resolved.

Assuming, however, that we manage to keep our basic right to sue reasonably intact, will it continue to be subject to occasional abuse? Undoubtedly—just as the right to freedom of expression guaranteed to us under the First Amendment will go on being used to express opinions that are venomous, unjust or plain ridiculous.

But keep in mind that should anyone misuse their right to speak freely by spreading malicious lies that impact your reputation, you would still have the option of responding with an "action of defamation."

Author's note: The "Lily Ledbetter Act" was one of the first pieces of legislation signed into law by President Obama upon taking office in 2009.

A LESSON IN REALITY FROM TODAY'S 'MAD MEN'

(Originally published in The SandPaper, August 2010)

In an episode from a previous season of AMC's blockbuster hit show "Mad Men," Peter Campbell, the brash and ambitious young account executive for Sterling Cooper, the 1960s-era Madison Avenue ad agency around which the series revolves, has a eureka moment. Looking over sales figures for one of the agency's clients, Admiral televisions (the series may be fictitious, but the scriptwriters use real companies), he realizes that the only locales where the product appears to be selling well are urban areas largely populated by what were then referred to as Negroes.

This sudden demographic epiphany prompts Campbell to make a daring recommendation. During a meeting with the client's representatives, he advises them to put a large portion of their advertising into magazines such as *Ebony* and *Jet* in order to deliberately target and cultivate that Negro market.

Instead of being impressed by Campbell's insight, however, the reps are downright offended by the idea of having their products known as the TV sets most favored by people of color. And he subsequently gets a dressing down from the higher-ups at Sterling Cooper, who want to know what on earth he could have been thinking in making so indiscreet a suggestion.

What may have struck some ad agency execs and clients as a rash and boat-rocking strategy back in an era when the civil rights movement was just getting its act together, however, is now very much mainstream thinking in today's ad biz. To appreciate just how important the idea of targeting minority markets has become, in fact, one need look no further than the July 26 edition of *Advertising Age*, the industry bible.

"Count on it: Hispanic market hits tipping point," reads the headline over one of its front-page stories, along with the subhead: "Demo accounts for one in six U.S. residents. Nearly half are at ease in English." Inside the same publication is a 46-page supplementary booklet: the 2010 edition of its "Hispanic Fact Pack," described as an "Annual Guide to Hispanic Marketing and Media."

All of that brings back to mind my own motivations in initially opting for a career in journalism rather than advertising.

It so happens that I view "Mad Men" as more than just an intriguing television drama, or one that reflects the mores of a certain time. Having had an ad executive stepfather who constantly hobnobbed and drank with the Madison Avenue crowd of that particular era, I grew up with first-hand exposure to the types of people depicted in the show.

My familiarity with their world became further amplified when, as a high-school senior, I attended the convention of the Advertising Federation of America in Denver to accept a trophy and $500 savings bond as first-prize winner in the organization's 1962 essay contest on the subject of "Advertising and the Free World." (I think the line that clinched it was "Advertising is the voice of free enterprise.") My winning essay was written up in several papers, including the New York *Journal American*, and resulted in my being extended a number of prospective invitations from various VIPs on the agency scene to come see them once I got out of college. Those were contacts that might have proved valuable had I chosen to pursue them.

But I didn't. The truth was an advertising career didn't interest me in the least, and I had entered that contest only because I had been required to do so as part of a high-school course in journalism, which was my real passion at the time.

In retrospect, I think the thing that most attracted me to a low-paying career in the newspaper business, rather than the much more lucrative opportunity to become a member of the gray-flannel-suit set, was my desire to get involved in what I regarded as the real issues of the day, seeking truth and exposing its opposite. By contrast, advertising looked to me like a phony-baloney, constricted, and somewhat amoral enterprise whose only objective was to find clever or coercive ways to make people want to buy stuff they often didn't need.

While I eventually found myself in the business of writing ad copy for small agencies as well as working as a reporter and editor, I still harbor many of those same feelings toward both lines of endeavor. Only now, I'm having to somewhat re-evaluate which field is actually the one most grounded in reality.

Pick up any newspaper today, or at least any that's still around, and what you see being reported are reflections of contemporary xenophobia—attempts in various communities to make Hispanic immigrants distinctly unwelcome, for instance, or public opinion polls showing support for measures aimed at making it easier to identify and deport those here without documentation, such as the law recently passed in Arizona.

What such "news" actually does, however, is to help reinforce a fear-fueled opposition to a fundamental change in the demographics of our country. It's not all that different, in fact, from the massive resistance during the 1950s and '60s—and not just in the South—to Afro-Americans being recognized as first-class citizens of the republic, which actually ran counter to the laws of many states back then.

Pick up *Advertising Age*, however, and you feel like you've suddenly made a bold leap into the future, where such change is already an accomplished and accepted fact of life, much as the presence of black people now is in our professional and political spheres (which isn't to say that bias against them has been totally eliminated from American society by any means).

Nowhere in the publication, for instance, is there any mention of the "illegals" on which media coverage of the Hispanic influx has largely focused, but only a discussion of its "transformative effect on the U.S. culture, including music, food and sports, as illustrated by this year's World Cup fervor." Nor is there any reference to the threat Latinos are widely believed to pose to traditional American values that is so often echoed in news reporting. Instead, the emphasis is on "how closely they exemplify our concept of 1950s America," with "large, traditional married-with-children families" and "lots of participation from grandparents," on how they eat meals at home, "spend less than average on alcohol," and "tend to be community-oriented and have high aspirations for their children."

Thus, while the news media continually remind us how many Americans regard this latest wave of immigrants as alien invaders, stealing both jobs and welfare benefits and helping push us toward economic collapse, the "Mad Men" of today view them as trendsetters who, according to *Advertising Age*, will be playing a "major role" in keeping the retail sector healthy as baby boomers retire and curtail their spending.

The ad biz, to be sure, has been the subject of a great deal of well-deserved criticism. Manipulative by its very nature, it has often used its powers of persuasion for less than beneficial purposes or to hype harmful products, such as those ubiquitous cigarettes, the smoking of which a Sterling Cooper employee referred to as practically a requirement of working there.

But then, just like such flawed "Mad Men" characters as Peter Campbell and the show's protagonist, Creative Director Don Draper, the huckstering trade can suddenly rise above its ignoble inclinations and prove itself capable of exemplary behavior. And nowhere is such behavior more evident than in the way it has acknowledged and adapted itself to the realities of a changing American ethnic landscape.

It's just a shame that an understanding so profoundly important is confined to a journal disseminated mainly among industry insiders. It should be released as a public service message by the one group that would know how to make Americans aware that the cultural transition so many are now resisting has already taken place, at least as far as the free-enterprise system is concerned.

A NEW BUMPER-STICKER SENTIMENT FOR SITUATIONS WHEN PUSH COMES TO SHOVEL

(Originally published in The Philadelphia Inquirer, January 2011)

At the start of both a new year and decade, much of the conversation here in New Jersey seems to have remained mired in the last week of the old one—specifically on why those assigned the job of digging us out of a deep fiscal hole weren't more proficient at digging us out from under the Zhivago-size snowfall that buried much of the Eastern Seaboard the day after Christmas.

It's easy enough, of course, to dump on Governor Christie and his second-in-command for having been absent from their command posts during the unforeseen emergency. (That both chose to visit tourist destinations in balmier climes instead of being home for the holidays, however, doesn't exactly bespeak a "New Jersey state of mind.") Or to blame New York Mayor Mike Bloomberg for the fact that so many of his city's residents remained snowbound for days after the blizzard.

But while these fallible humans are being taken to task for failing to stay one step ahead of Mother Nature, no such culpability seems to have attached itself to our supposedly far more competent computer systems.

I'm referring to the fact that a mere two days prior to the arrival of this monster nor'easter, "all computer models" were reportedly "in agreement" that whatever storm was on the way would harmlessly blow out to sea before reaching our vicinity—resulting in predictions for that Sunday being changed from the possibility of snow to a merely cloudy outlook. In fact, it wasn't until Christmas Eve that we began to hear reports that the data on which those computer models had based their conclusions might have been a wee bit faulty.

But then, there was little reason for anyone in these parts to anticipate a full-blown nor'easter—at least, not if they had been listening to what some professional prognosticators were saying about prospects for the coming season.

Take, for example, the relatively bland long-range winter forecast made at the end of November by Philadelphia meteorologist Glenn "Hurricane" Schwartz. According to his analysis of historical weather-system patterns combined with all the latest data, conditions this year were anything but favorable for storms to "redevelop along the East Coast and become monster nor'easters." That, in his opinion, meant there would be "even less snow than in an average winter"—and "no huge snowstorms."

All of which suggests that despite our current levels of high-tech wizardry, we are still very much at the mercy of the elements. In other words, we can no more allow ourselves the luxury of completely relying on what those computers tell us than we can on the promises made by the officeholders we hire to keep our trains running on time, our budgets balanced and our roads cleared.

So on whom or what, then, can we depend when push comes to shove—or shovel—in a crisis? Let me offer an anecdotal answer.

When I attempted to venture outdoors on the night of the blizzard, I found I was unable to push the front screen door open, and realized we were quite literally snowed in. But by the next morning, the walkways in our condo complex were completely passable, the snow having been removed by a team of hardy Hispanic workers whom my sister observed braving frigid wind chills to clear them when she awoke at about 4:30 a.m. (one of whom, she noticed, wasn't even wearing gloves).

Now, I certainly can't say—nor do I care—whether or not all of those stalwart, shovel-ready individuals had "papers" giving them official permission to be here. But I do know that if some politicians had their way, many of the workers who are quite willing and able to tackle such rigorous situations would be sent packing—most likely back to Mexico, the very place where Lt. Gov. Kim Guadagno was vacationing while much of New Jersey was being buried under a couple feet of snow.

And that puts me in mind of an old right-wing bumper sticker that went: "If you don't trust the police, the next time you're in trouble, call a hippie." In fact, I'd like to offer my own, updated version of that sentiment: "If you're in favor of deporting undocumented laborers, the next time you find yourself snowed in, call a politician."

That is, assuming there are any around.

AN OFFICIAL STAMP OF APPROVAL FOR AN UNOFFICIAL STATUE OF LIBERTY

*(Originally published in The Philadelphia Inquirer and
The Record of Bergen County, N.J., April 2011)*

The depiction of a knock-off Statue of Liberty on the U.S. Postal Service's new "forever" stamp has been called a "case of mistaken identity." But I can't help thinking that the substitution of a Las Vegas casino's replica for the actual icon in New York Harbor couldn't be more symbolically suited to the U.S.A. of today.

A century ago, that welcoming statue might well have represented the aspirations of those tired, poor, huddled masses yearning to breathe free, who believed this country offered everyone a chance to strive for a decent standard of living. To be sure, after stepping off the boat, many of these "tempest-tost" folks soon found themselves exploited by factory owners and living in squalid tenements. But unlike the places they fled, America offered opportunity and optimism—the proverbial promise of a better life for those who could work their way out of poverty. And many succeeded in doing just that (my Russian-born grandparents among them).

So important was that promise that when the country found itself in the throes of an unprecedented economic collapse, the government put millions back to work revitalizing its infrastructure and creating public works that remained viable for decades.

Today, however, that sense of potential has been significantly downsized, along with the security that once came with middle-class status and the opportunities to perform productive work of any kind. There is perhaps no better reflection of the latter than the thousands of applicants who recently showed up for a shot at low-wage jobs at McDonald's, indicating that the "golden door" Lady Liberty lifted her lamp beside has now been replaced by the golden arches.

REPEAT OFFENDERS

So it's only fitting that the statue represented on the first-class stamp—the one adorning Las Vegas' *New York–New York* Hotel and Casino—is only half the size of the real McCoy. Rather than a renowned beacon to immigrants seeking a new world of opportunity, it's an ersatz monument to the masses huddled in front of slot machines, the majority of which will leave somewhat poorer—and probably more tired—than when they arrived.

The Postal Service's mistake might not have been so accidentally apt if what happened in Vegas had actually stayed in Vegas. But over the past few years, the casino culture spawned by that city has spread to the far corners of the land, coinciding with the American dream's transformation from being one's due for diligence into a prize in a vast game of chance.

This substitution for one of the country's most venerated symbols has been blessed by none other than the U.S. government itself, as reflected in a statement issued by postal spokesman Roy Betts: "We still love the stamp design and would have selected this photograph anyway." Thus has a stamp of approval been given to this new symbol of America as a society of winners and losers, in which a lucky few get to take home some of the highest-paying jackpots in history while many more end up losing their shirts.

So while this official use of an unofficial Statue of Liberty may have been unintended, we now have three billion reminders of what its torch of freedom actually stands for: not the pursuit of happiness traditionally associated with a job or career suited to one's abilities, but the right to risk one's money on a toss of the dice or a shot at the lottery.

Speaking of which, it might be a good idea to stock up on those "forever" stamps while you have the chance, because the only sure bet left in America is that the price of postage will keep rising.

ACKNOWLEDGMENTS

I have had the pleasure of working with a number of op-ed and commentary editors during the quarter century in which the essays contained in this collection were being prepared for initial publication, all of whom helped keep them suitable for newspaper audiences and "on message." Perhaps my longest such relationship has been with Gail Travers, executive editor of *The SandPaper*, who has indulged at least 98 percent of my rhetorical flights of fancy and the occasional offense I have given to readers (and, on one or two occasions, advertisers) over more than two decades, and patiently turned many of my inordinately long sentences into shorter, more readable grammatical entities (but not without first bringing such excesses to my attention).

Other editors who have elected to publish these pieces and helped guide the process include (in no particular order) Bill Everhart, Mary Grace Butler (who has remained a friend over many years) and Tad Ames at *The Berkshire Eagle;* Josh Gohlke, Porus Cooper, Dave Boyer, Jodie Chester, Janet McMillan and Harold Jackson at *The Philadelphia Inquirer;* Peter Grad at *The Record* of Bergen County, and Michael Murphy at the *Orlando Sentinel.*

At Divertir, I would like to thank editor Laura Jamison for pointing out where these essays might be further improved (including breaking up some more of those aforementioned long sentences) or updated in author's notes, and Dr. Kenneth Tupper for recognizing the potential of this collection, despite not having received it through the intermediary of an agent.

I would also like to thank my sister Linda Bonvie, a first-rate blogger and long-time collaborator on health and environmental topics, for her ideas and suggestions that helped to enhance many of these essays, and to extend a special note of appreciation to my good friend (and former classmate) Ginny Rorby, the author of several superlative young adult novels, who critiqued the original version of the "Backward" and otherwise provided me with encouragement in this project.

Finally, I want to thank my college journalism instructor and mentor Ted Hargrove, from whom I learned the various and sundry aspects of being a good reporter—and to avoid clichés like the plague.

ABOUT THE AUTHOR

Bill Bonvie is a freelance writer whose experience includes having worked as a reporter and editor for various newspapers and as a copywriter for advertising agencies. The subject matter for this book has all been drawn from the numerous opinion and commentary pieces he has had published over the past three decades in such newspapers as *The Philadelphia Inquirer*, *The Berkshire Eagle*, *The Orlando Sentinel*, and *The Record* of Bergen County, N.J., as well as in *The SandPaper*, a free weekly newsmagazine serving southern Ocean County, N.J. He has also co-authored both books and numerous magazine and newspaper articles on health and environmental topics in collaboration with his sister Linda Bonvie (including an article that led to more than 20 countries dropping the practice of spraying passengers on arriving flights with a toxic pesticide), and serves as editor of the Chemical-Free Kids Facebook page.

www.ingramcontent.com/pod-product-compliance
Lightning Source LLC
Chambersburg PA
CBHW052024070526
44584CB00016B/1896